POETIC REMAKING
The Art of Browning, Yeats, and Pound

POETIC REMAKING
The Art of Browning, Yeats, and Pound

George Bornstein

THE PENNSYLVANIA STATE UNIVERSITY PRESS
University Park and London

Library of Congress Cataloging-in-Publication Data

Bornstein, George.
  Poetic remaking.

  Bibliography: p.
  Includes index.
  1. English poetry—19th century—History and
criticism.   2. English poetry—20th century—History
and criticism.   3. Browning, Robert, 1812–1889—
Technique.   4. Yeats, W. B. (William Butler),
1865–1939—Technique.   5. Pound, Ezra, 1885–1972—
Technique.   6. Literary form.   7. Influence (Literary,
artistic, etc.) I. Title.
PR591.B58   1988   821'.8'09   87-25789
ISBN 0-271-00620-X

For Rebecca

"That all her thoughts may like the linnet be"

Contents

Preface

The nine essays composing this volume offer a coherent though necessarily selective view of postromantic poetic development in terms both of individual poems and of poetic influence. They focus most centrally on Browning in the Victorian period and on Yeats and Pound in the modern, but they also look more briefly at works by Wordsworth, Coleridge, Keats, Arnold, Tennyson, and Eliot.

The introductory manifesto, "Four Gaps in Postromantic Influence Study," posits four new orientations for such work: taking the volume (rather than the individual poem) as unit; stressing more centrally the Victorian mediation between romantic and modern; emphasizing national differences among English, Irish, and American traditions as well as the potential importance within them of a foreign poet like Dante; and basing influence studies as much on manuscript materials as on finished products. Each of the following chapters follows one or more of those orientations.

The main body of the book includes two groups of studies. The first group of four, "Remaking Poetry," focuses on readings of specific poetic texts. The initial chapter in this section treats Browning's first major volume as a unit; the second reads his dramatic monologue "Pictor Ignotus" against romantic acts of mind; the third maps distinctively Victorian variations in the major form known as Greater Romantic Lyric; and the fourth explores Yeats's mature revision of that form.

The second group of four chapters, "Remaking Poets," stresses the dynamics of literary influence by which poets turn their forerunners into figures helpful to their own development. The first three chapters examine Yeats's encounters with Dante, with Spenser, and with Browning and Tennyson, respectively; the fourth treats Pound's remaking of the poet he called his poetic "father," Browning, in a way that suggests the limits of anxiety models of poetic influence.

The book originated in a larger number of essays published over the past ten years. I have selected those that best fit together, written a new essay (on the Greater Victorian Lyric), drastically revised the opening chapter on the "Four Gaps," and made numerous smaller changes throughout the volume. The revised essays are used here with permission of the original publishers. Chapter 1 first appeared in *Romanticism Past and Present* 6,2 (1982): 1–9; Chapter 2 in *Poems in Their Place: The Intertextuality and Order of Poetic Collections,* ed. Neil Fraistat (© University of North Carolina Press, 1986); Chapter 3 in *Victorian Poetry* 19 (1981): 65–72; Chapter 5 in *Romantic and Modern: Revaluations of Literary Tradition,* ed. George Bornstein (University of Pittsburgh Press, 1977); Chapter 6 in *Colby Library Quarterly* 15 (1979): 93–113 and *Dante Among the Moderns,* ed. Stuart Y. McDougal (© University of North Carolina Press, 1985); Chapter 7 in *Yeats: An Annual of Critical and Textual Studies,* Volume II—1984, ed. Richard J. Finneran (© Cornell University Press, 1984); Chapter 8 in *Yeats Annual No. 1,* ed. Richard J. Finneran (The Macmillan Press, 1982); and Chapter 9 in *Ezra Pound Among the Poets,* ed. George Bornstein (© University of Chicago Press, 1985).

Quotations from the works of Ezra Pound are used by permission of the publishers, New Directions Publishing Corporation and Faber & Faber, Limited: *The Cantos of Ezra Pound* (Copyright © 1934, 1937, 1940, 1948, 1956, 1959, 1962, 1963, 1965, 1968, 1970 by Ezra Pound); *Personae* (Copyright © 1926 by Ezra Pound); excerpts from letters and manuscripts (Copyright © 1984 by the Trustees of the Ezra Pound Literary Property Trust).

Quotations from the poems of W. B. Yeats are used by permission of the Macmillan Publishing Company from *The Variorum Edition of the Poems of W. B. Yeats,* ed. Peter Allt and Russell K. Alspach. Copyright 1918, 1924, 1928, 1933 by Macmillan Publishing Company, renewed 1946, 1952, 1956, 1961 by Bertha Georgie Yeats. Copyright 1940 by Georgie Yeats, renewed 1968 by Bertha Georgie Yeats, Michael Butler Yeats, and Anne Yeats.

Thomas Parkinson and Richard Finneran offered useful and sympathetic suggestions for improving an earlier version of the volume, while Richard Badenhausen assisted in preparing the final copy. Thomas Collins, John Maynard, and Chip Tucker all helped to tutor me in Browning. The College of Literature, Science, and Arts and the Research Partnership Program of the University of Michigan both provided support. My wife Jane made this book as well as much else possible, and my son Ben lent encouragement. I cannot say that my two-year-old daughter Rebecca contributed anything specific to the making of this volume, but her presence has been a joy. I inscribe *Poetic Remaking* to her in the hope that, when she learns to read, she will take pleasure in the fact that her father once dedicated a book to her.

1 Introduction: Four Gaps in Postromantic Influence Study

A famous Irish-American lawyer and patron of the arts in New York, John Quinn, once told a group of respectable bankers a ribald story which eventually found its way into *The Cantos* of Ezra Pound. Because of its suggestiveness for the study of poetic influence, and because Quinn himself fostered so many modernist interactions, I begin with his account of the Honest Sailor, as rendered by Pound. In it a drunken sailor is tricked into believing that he has given birth to a son, whereupon he reforms and raises the boy on his own, only to confess on his deathbed that he is not the true father:

> Said Jim X . . . :
> There once was a pore honest sailor, a heavy drinker,
> A hell of a cuss, a rowster, a boozer, and
> The drink finally sent him to hospital,
> And they operated, and there was a poor whore in
> The woman's ward had a kid, while
> They were fixing the sailor, and they brought him the kid
> When he came to, and said:
> "Here! this is what we took out of you."
>
> An' he looked at it, an' he got better,
> And when he left the hospital, quit the drink,
> And when he was well enough
>   signed on with another ship
> And saved up his pay money,
>   and kept on savin' his pay money,

And bought a share in the ship,
   and finally had half shares,
Then a ship
   and in time a whole line of steamers;
And educated the kid,
   and when the kid was in college,
The ole sailor was again taken bad
   and the doctors said he was dying,
And the boy came to the bedside,
   and the old sailor said:
"Boy, I'm sorry I can't hang on a bit longer,
"You're young yet.
   I leave you re-sponsa-bilities.
"Wish I could ha' waited till you were older,
"More fit to take over the bisness . . ."
   "But, father,
"Don't, don't talk about me, I'm all right,
"It's you, father."
   "That's it, boy, you said it.
"You called me your father, and I ain't.
"I ain't your dad, no,
"I am not your fader but your moder," quod he,
"Your fader was a rich merchant in Stambouli."[1]

We may have even more trouble than the Honest Sailor in tracing the complicated genesis of a work of art. Current thought directs us either toward the author or toward other texts. Yet like the Honest Sailor, the author nurtures the work of art but always skews its lineage, and secretly imagines himself its mother even while playing his fatherly role. And while other texts come into play, ultimately they may engender even less than does the Stambouli merchant. Before returning eventually to the third parental candidate in Quinn's fable, I should like first to ponder four gaps in the literary history we construct for the products of such problematic ancestry.

Fifteen years ago, few scholars expected problems of influence to fill a large role in formulating new approaches to romantic and postromantic poetry. Until then, influence study figured less as a new direction than as a backward loop in literary scholarship. With a few honorable exceptions, "influence" inspired thoughts of dry source studies or

Quellenforschungen, with their long lists of similar passages; of reputation studies, with their reportorial chroniclings of "reception"; or of literary propagandists eager, say, to boost the modernism of Eliot and Pound by displacing the Romantics with the metaphysicals as models. All three approaches led to stasis. Both writers and their works acquired a stable identity which permitted the individual talent to realign the ideal order among the monuments of tradition but masked their and his instability.

Influence study became interesting when it became dynamic. Newer theories replace synchronic with diachronic modes which chart the relation of influence to change over a career. They stress distortion of the forerunner over similarity as a way of identifying uniqueness. Most important of all, they replace the stable (or primary) model of the self or oeuvre with a more problematic (or antithetical) one, often with analogy to internalized family romance.[2] All writers become like Quinn's Honest Sailor. Even if in one of our New England seaports the anxiety of influence sometimes looks more like the influence of anxiety, these changes have moved consideration of influence to the front of our discipline and are one of the most vigorous products of the general revival of romanticism. At present, two trends predominate: One stresses an "intertextuality" underpinned by contemporary French theory, and the other adapts more traditional Anglo-American attitudes. My own work obviously belongs to the second category. Yet I should like to identify here four "gaps" which exist in both camps and which need attention by each as it formulates new approaches to the study of postromantic poetry, and particularly to the nature of poetic influence. The first two gaps affect notions of literary history; and the second two, definition of the "text" itself.

The very first gap concerns the great Victorian poets, a phrase which until fairly recently might have struck many non-Victorianists as a contradiction in terms. As Samuel Butler remarked even during Tennyson's lifetime, "We said we knew Blake was no good because he learnt Italian at 60 in order to study Dante, and we knew Dante was no good because he ran Virgil, and we knew Virgil was no good because Tennyson ran him, and as for Tennyson—well, he went without saying."[3] Modernism and the New Criticism completed the reaction begun by Butler and others, and even the postwar romantic rehabilitation skipped over Tennyson, Arnold, and Browning as a sort of disloyal opposition in the history of English poetry. That chronological quarantine shows signs of breaking down. For the first half of the nineteenth century, recent interest in Victorian romanticism has inspired new respect for the chief Victorians, though we still tend to see them too much as lapsed Romantics, a series of failed Childe Rolands. At the other end of the period, however, we have not yet overcome the modernist myth of a sharp break with the nineteenth century which obscures underlying continuities. Carol Christ's recent linkage of Victorian and modern doctrines of mask, theories of images, and constructs of myth and history offers a sustained argument for how we might do so.[4]

Two kinds of links preoccupy me here. First comes direct influence. "Überhaupt ich stamm aus Browning. Pourquoi nier son père?" (Generally, I come from Browning. Why deny one's father?) writes Pound, like the dutiful son of the Honest Sailor.[5] Critics have traced Pound's filial use of the dramatic monologue, manipulation of persona, historical setting, and even specific phrasing (to understand why Pound associated Keats with a murex, we need to know why Browning did so in his poem "Popularity").[6] None has braved the full impact of *Sordello* on *The Cantos*, perhaps because that would involve mastering the most obscure poem in each of two centuries, and none has traced the full shape of Pound's family romance with Browning. Neither have we appreciated the relation of Eliot's career to Tennyson's, although Eliot's portrait of Tennyson in the *In Memoriam* essay as "the most instinctive rebel against the society in which he was the most perfect conformist" suggests the kind of kinship between them, as A. Walton Litz has implied.[7]

Second comes the common problem of wrestling with romanticism. The careers of major postromantic poets on both sides of the water show a central and pervasive coming to terms with their forerunners, often in a three-stage series running from early imitation through intermediate repudiation to final reconciliation. The resultant patterns connect their later careers to those both of the Romantics and of each other. I take an example not from across the Atlantic, but only from across the Irish Sea. In the last stanza of his 1938 lyric "Are You Content?" William Butler Yeats writes,

> Infirm and aged I might stay
> In some good company,
> I who have always hated work,

> Smiling at the sea,
> Or demonstrate in my own life
> What Robert Browning meant
> By an old hunter talking with Gods;
> But I am not content.[8]

As I argue in Chapter 8, it is not enough here to know that Browning's image of the old hunter talking with gods comes from *Pauline,* where it represents the clarity and intensity of vicarious experience offered by literature to the Browning-like narrator. We must also recollect that *Pauline* explicitly chronicles Browning's early relation to Shelley, the same poet who Yeats claimed shaped his own life. With partial truth, Yeats saw the rest of Browning's reaction as a progression from the "subjective" to the "objective" poet of Browning's own essay on Shelley, which Yeats judged the most "philosophic . . . fundamental and radical" work of modern criticism.[9] Only Yeats thought—or needed to think—that Browning had sacrificed his own youthful subjectivity to an objective masking that degenerated into mere psychological curiosity. Yeats himself increasingly sought to move downwards upon objective life, but without betraying the subjective vision of his youth. He repeatedly cited the *Pauline* passage as an example of the simplified intensity appropriate for the mask of antithetical artists like himself. Hence, "Are You Content?" both chides Browning for reacting against Shelley in the wrong way and establishes Yeats's own adherence to the continual questing for images of concentrated intensity which defined his own poetic maturity. That devotion saved him both from becoming only a diminutive Shelley and from merely repeating the terms of Browning's prior reaction, with which Yeats was not content.

The following essays explore both forms of Victorian connection. Those in Part One focus on specific major poems by Browning, Tennyson, Arnold, Yeats, and Eliot as individual responses to the Greater Romantic Lyric. Each later poet exploited that genre both to adapt romanticism and to establish his independence from it. The first three essays in Part Two examine more direct influences on Yeats. Sometimes he sought to free himself from the original Romantics by projecting onto earlier writers like Dante or Spenser a corrected romanticism embodying his own poetic aims. At other times, his critiques of Browning and Tennyson reveal his desire to remake romanticism without becoming a mere copyist of previous Victorian adaptations. The final essay establishes Pound's early devotion to and later absorption of Browning in terms of his own Browning-like understanding of poetic influence in a model sometimes at odds with current theories of poetic anxiety.

Paying attention to literary history might lead us to pay more attention to history itself. Too often influence theory has worked in a social vacuum, as though a culture consisted only of poetry and philosophy. Even the most virulently anti-Eliotic of modern critics still talk and write as though the monuments of the past really did form an ideal order only among themselves. One subset of broader historical concern would be discrimination of cross-cultural influences even within Western tradition, which has more elements of contested plurality than some recent opponents of hierarchical hegemony lead us to believe. My two chief modern examples so far—Pound and Yeats—were not English. Postromantic influence involves the impact of the English Romantics and Victorians on their foreign successors, whether Irish or American. This complicates the role of the forerunner as progenitor. "Creative work has always a father*land*," wrote Yeats under the sobriquet "The Celt in London" in a column for an American newspaper. Its readers could be expected to understand and sympathize with his cultural plight, mirroring as it did their own. The year before, he had told still other American readers that "one can only reach out to the universe with a gloved hand—that glove is one's nation, the only thing one knows even a little of."[10]

The crucial awareness of English poets as foreigners which pervades nineteenth-century American studies mysteriously evaporates in the modern period, whose scholars tend to follow Eliot, Pound, and perhaps Henry James in thinking of England and Europe as more refined civilizations. To our nineteenth-century poets the Romantics and Victorians appeared as adversaries more to national than to personal development. When in 1832 Longfellow berated American writers for having "imbibed the degenerate spirit of modern English poetry," when in 1847 Whitman denounced "servile . . . imitation of London," and when in 1869 Lowell declared that "we are worth nothing except so far as we have disinfected ourselves of Anglicism," they fought for the character of an entire culture and infused internal individual revolt with the dialectics of national liberation.[11] So, too,

did the Irish, on the other side of the water. Yeats admired the vener-
able Fenian hero John O'Leary for having "seen that there is no fine
nationality without literature, and seen the converse also, that there is
no fine literature without nationality."[12] The American men of letters
Nathaniel Willis and George P. Morris, who had declared in the 1840s
that "the country is tired of being *be-Britished,*" would have applauded
the Irish Douglas Hyde's ringing 1892 inaugural address to the new
National Literary Society on "The Necessity for De-Anglicising Ire-
land." The subtlest recent analyst of the American cultural struggle
with England during the nineteenth century, Robert Weisbuch, has
demonstrated that the nationalist proponents may be divided into two
schools: a "party of mimesis," who championed the use of specifically
American materials ("the Hudson for the Thames, the Catskills for
Mount Olympus"); and a "party of consciousness," who favored a
distinctively American approach to more cosmopolitan materials.[13] As
Weisbuch points out, proponents of either side of that bifurcation can
seem naive, and a true recovery of what Henry James called the saving
secret depended upon a fusion of both in the same writer. That happens
in Yeats, too, who has a foot in the camps of both mimesis (in
Weisbuch's sense) and consciousness, and in the best work of Ezra
Pound as well.

Such intercultural dynamics did not disappear in the early twentieth
century, though they rarely surface in influence studies of the modern-
ist generation. But merely being English (as opposed to American or
Irish) affected the reception of romantic tradition. In turn-of-the-
century America, with cultural independence by then more secure,
they offered grandparental alternatives: Their very foreignness offered
room for maneuver. To Wallace Stevens the gods of China were
Chinese, the natives of the rain were rainy men, and all he did came
from Pennsylvania and Connecticut. Like one of the nineteenth-
century party of mimesis, this arch-poet of consciousness could declare
that "The image must be of the nature of its creator / . . . Wood of his
forests and stone out of his fields / Or from under his mountains."[14] In
Ireland, with national identity still more problematic, English poets
seemed more ambiguous. Yet Yeats, too, favored localism, bemoaned
the richness lost to Shelley and Blake by inadequate national my-
thologies, and sought to correct romanticism by fastening it to the Irish
countryside:

> Might I not, with health and good luck to aid me, create some new *Prometheus Unbound;* Patrick or Columcille, Oisin or Finn, in Prometheus' stead; and, instead of Caucasus, Cro-Patrick or Ben Bulben? Have not all races had their first unity from a mythology that marries them to rock and hill?[15]

Correspondingly, from early poems like "To Ireland in the Coming Times" to late ones like "The Statues" he sought to locate Irishness as much in consciousness as in geography, creating an Irish analogue to James's American secret. This national orientation permitted last romantics like Stevens and Yeats (or for that matter Crane and Frost) to embrace their romantic predecessors and yet claim to have revised them by adapting them to the poetry of other climates. In contrast, cosmopolitans like Eliot and sometimes Pound would attack the Romantics and the modern regionalists, even while producing a cosmopolitan poetry somehow instantly recognizable as American.

Cross-cultural factors affect poetic influence in one other way as well. Poets who wrote in a different language can liberate later poets from the intimidations of their own immediate predecessors in their own language. Thus, Yeats turns to Dante partly to free himself from Shelley and Blake, making the Italian poet into an idealized corrective whose influence did not threaten loss of individuality. More broadly, the relentlessly polyglot searches of Ezra Pound allowed him to schematize his own poetic tradition as including Italian poets like Dante, classical ones like Homer or Ovid, and Chinese ones like Li Po. In so doing, he rid himself of the anxiety besetting more monolingual poets measuring themselves against a line deriving from Milton. Insecure national identity can lead to projection of an anxiety model onto a cultural context, but more secure traditions can make international experience more enabling than threatening. We have barely begun to appreciate the dark italics of nationalism to the development of postromantic poetry.

In charting the interrelations of that poetry, criticism has not queried carefully enough what unit to choose as "text." For all its sophistication about that key word in modern theory, criticism—when it does not equate text with all of literature, or even in more madcap versions with all of life—still uses it to designate either the individual work or the whole of a writer's oeuvre. We ponder the influence of

"Shelley" on "Yeats," or of Keats's "To Autumn" upon Stevens's "Sunday Morning"; sometimes we cross the two categories and speak of "Whitman's" response to "the romantic crisis poem." I should like to propose a third possibility—the volume. Throughout the period, poets have industriously arranged their work in individual volumes, whose implications we too often ignore. More comprehensive than the isolated lyric and more limited and unified than the collected works, the volume stands at once as both source of influence and response to it.

The practice of unifying books of poetry runs from the Hellenistic book rolls of classical antiquity to the present day and includes both the three major poets of the present study and the predecessors who influenced them. The same Callimachus whom Pound invokes at the start of *Homage to Sextus Propertius*, for example, was the first Western poet to advise the reader about the shape of his canon and to employ sophisticated techniques for unifying his individual books. The more modern tradition begins with Dante in the *Vita Nuova* and Petrarch in the *Canzoniere*, poets well known to Yeats, Pound, and Browning, and in English extends from the Renaissance sonneteers through Spenser and Milton to the great Romantics. In the romantic and Victorian periods, as Neil Fraistat has reminded us in his important explorations, the practice of unifying individual volumes was both widespread and explicit.[16] Yeats, for example, would have found careful and complex ordering in Blake's *Songs of Innocence and of Experience* or Shelley's *Prometheus Unbound, with Other Poems*.

Our great modern editions lead us to distort how writers actually encountered each other. Sometimes they confronted collected editions arranged on shelves like armies of unalterable law, but more often they picked up individual volumes, and even nineteenth-century collected editions sometimes kept the original demarcations. A later poet might respond not to all of Keats chronologically arranged, but, say, to the volume entitled *Lamia, Isabella, The Eve of St. Agnes, and Other Poems*. That book contained the great odes, and we read them better for placing them in a progression from the opening *Lamia*, where Lycius pursues an illusory ideal opposed to life, to the concluding *Hyperion*, where Apollo dies into life. Similarly, Browning's rearrangement of *Men and Women* calls attention to the plan of its contents. Later poets often specify their response to such books as units. In his essay "T. S. Eliot," for example, Pound observes that "the most interesting poems in Victorian English are Browning's *Men and Women*"; furthermore, Pound's essay itself is not a full-fledged one on Eliot at all, but rather a review of the *Prufrock* volume.[17]

Fraistat has coined the term "contextual poetics" to describe the reading of a volume in terms of "the 'poem' that is the book itself."[18] Such an approach not only includes a range of forms, themes, and patterns but also provides a means of rehistoricizing texts by returning them to a context (the volume) that occupies a particular place in its own culture and society. The following essay on Browning's *Dramatic Lyrics* (1842) attempts just such a strategy. On the one hand, it studies the volume as a whole compounded of paired poems arranged in a coherent design punctuated by individual ones marking the chief turning points. Even the best-known poems from that book, like "My Last Duchess," gain new significance when viewed in their original literary context. On the other hand, the essay argues strongly for the deliberate relation of the volume to political events in the England of 1842, a social context which disappears if we neglect the original arrangement.

Besides shaping the reading of individual poems or volumes, contextual poetics should modify our conclusions about influence as well. A lyric like "Are You Content?" has both a specific context and a role within that context. Yeats arranged his volumes with particular care, often as a progression from a falsely attractive austerity to a more human stance. He gave "Are You Content?" special prominence by placing it as the final poem in his *New Poems* volume of 1938. There that lyric completes the movement downward upon life and humanity, away from the inhuman (and inhumane) glee with which the opening poem, "The Gyres," confronts history. Browning's image thus stands for an alternate route to Yeats's own back from apocalypse to individual men and women. In rejecting that route, Yeats embraces the imperfection of the life but keeps his own poetic identity. Conversely, the volume controls our response to the introductory lyric, "The Gyres." To condemn that poem for betraying romantic humanism—as one prominent critic of influence has done—misses the point that the volume itself already repudiates its opening position; it offers both critique and correction en route to its saving refusal to rest content.

If the volume expands the notion of text in one direction, the first draft does so in another. Surprisingly, influence studies rarely involve substantial use of manuscripts. Instead, they privilege the final version and unravel complexities of influence wholly from that. The procedure hardly makes sense. Surely the dynamics of influence show themselves most clearly first in the prior-unrevised-original beginning of the poem and then in successive revisions toward the final, published version. The canonical text represents the conclusion of a struggle rather than its inception or recapitulation; the antagonist, furthermore, may be more the blank page or chaotic first fillings of it than a previous poet. This principle extends as well to a poet's shaping of his entire canon. Yeats's successive revisings of his early canon, for example, increasingly excluded the political or topical works, until he finally arrived at a deliberately constructed beginning for his collected works which postponed political poems until after the turn of the century. For studies of poetic influence on the early Yeats, the social involvement of the original early canon demands attention.[19] It is the *poet's* self that he remakes.

Accordingly, I have employed manuscript materials when pertinent throughout these essays, particularly in those on Yeats and Spenser and most extensively in the one on Pound and Browning. There the original versions of poems like "Mesmerism" or the first three Cantos claim considerable attention. In addition, I have marshalled a range of other unpublished manuscript sources, including an early student notebook in which Pound himself derives a theory of poetic influence from Browning. In the case of Yeats, I have found his unpublished marginalia for his Spenser edition as helpful as the essay on Spenser originally published as the introduction to that volume. While according priority to eventually published versions of texts, such investigations do contest the absolute privileging of the final version which permeates most work on poetic influence of whatever camp. At the same time, watching the evolution of a text does tend to reinforce a sense of the author as subject and to make it harder to conceive of texts as self-generating.

The current slighting of manuscript materials results partly from a chief vice of theoretical contemporary criticism, its habit of construing figurative terms literally and literal ones figuratively. The vocabulary of "beginnings," "origins," "priority," "production," "initiation," and even "revision," for example, applies figuratively rather than literally, and such crossing of senses has generated some of the finest insights as well as silliest failures of academic criticism. It is even possible to have a distinguished book on literary beginnings which makes no use of manuscripts or literal beginnings. The high road of literary theory and the low road of textual scholarship seem never to meet. And yet they must.

Publication of Eliot's *Waste Land* manuscripts has forever enlarged our response to that poem and to its origins. Advanced scholarship on Joyce's *Ulysses* now centers on the extraordinary textual results of the Gabler edition. As it progresses, the Cornell Yeats series opens new vistas by printing successive manuscript drafts of the now-standard works. Such endeavors provide one potential bridge between current editorial and literary theory, for in different ways both disciplines call into question the old idea of the stable literary text and replace it with a less stable model.

By way of conclusion, I return to Quinn and Pound's anecdote of the Honest Sailor. Increased attention to Victorians and to volumes, to foreign cultures and to first drafts, will fill four gaps in influence study and literary history, but still will not solve the problem of the origins of creativity, or of its product the text. For that neither the Honest Sailor nor the Stambouli merchant, the alleged author or the texts he has encountered, will quite suffice. In desperation one turns to the third and neglected parent in the story, the poor harlot who did indeed give birth to the child. I propose to identify her in the same way that Yeats did a similar figure in the section of *A Vision* mischievously entitled "A Packet for Ezra Pound." There he wrote, "Muses resemble women who creep out at night and give themselves to unknown sailors and return to talk of Chinese porcelain . . . except that the Muses sometimes form in those low haunts their most lasting attachments."[20] Pound's harlot, like Yeats's women of the night, is of course the muse, the traditional parent of the literary text. She will continue to constitute a more satisfying explanation than all our contemporary study and theorizing, no matter how many gaps we fill.

PART ONE
Remaking Poetry

2 The Arrangement of Browning's *Dramatic Lyrics* (1842)

"It is an honourable distinction of Mr. Browning that in whatever he writes, you discover an *idea* of some sort or other," wrote Browning's early champion John Forster in his favorable review of the original *Dramatic Lyrics* for *The Examiner* in 1842. "There is purpose in all he does."[1] The early *Dramatic Lyrics* contained some of Browning's most famous short poems. As reviewer, Forster had an advantage over subsequent critics who usually encounter the poem in one of the later rearrangements by Browning or his editors. Forster necessarily took the volume as unit of his attention. As a result, he saw that Browning had designed the book around contrasting pairs of poems. His brief sketch of the pairs anticipated modern Browning criticism by over a hundred years, for only recently have scholars begun to grasp the importance of pairing in Browning's patterning of his verse.[2] Browning's overall concern for arrangement is well known, particularly as displayed in the 1863 reordering of the poems that had comprised *Dramatic Lyrics* (1842), *Dramatic Romances and Lyrics* (1845), and *Men and Women* (1855), and in the design of a later volume like *Dramatis Personae* (1864).[3] His most complexly structured work, *The Ring and the Book* (1868–69), consists of an intricate interlocking of related monologues. I should like to argue here that Browning's earliest collection of mature verse, *Dramatic Lyrics*, displays considerable architectonic skill in its deployment of paired poems punctuated by individual, free-standing ones. The pairs emphasize individual emotion in their thematic contrasts of love and its relation to moral or social law, while the independent poems reinforce the implicit contention of the pairs for a vital rather than antiquarian use of history by tying the collection to political events affecting the England of 1842.

A look at the original titles in the 1842 collection provides the best survey of its plan.[4] The poems appeared in this order:

Cavalier Tunes
    I. Marching Along
    II. Give a Rouse
    III. My Wife Gertrude [later called Boot and Saddle]
Italy and France
    I. Italy [later called My Last Duchess]
    II. France [later called Count Gismond]
Camp and Cloister
    I. Camp (French) [later called Incident of the French Camp]
    II. Cloister (Spanish) [later called Soliloquy of the Spanish
        Cloister]
In a Gondola
Artemis Prologuizes
Waring
Queen-Worship
    I. Rudel and [later, to] the Lady of Tripoli
    II. Cristina
Madhouse Cells
    I. [untitled; later called Johannes Agricola in Meditation]
    II. [untitled; later called Porphyria's Lover]
Through the Metidja to Abd-el-Kadr.—1842
The Pied Piper of Hamelin

While not joined by title, "In a Gondola" and "Artemis Prologuizes" form an obvious thematic pair based on death in illicit love, one quasi-historical and the other mythological. The volume thus runs from its opening triad of "Cavalier Tunes" through three related pairs to reach the independent "Waring" near the middle, and then presents two more related pairs en route to its original ending, "Through the Metidja to Abd-El-Kadr.—1842." Faced with his publisher Moxon's report that the collection as constituted was too short to fill the projected sixteen double-columned pages, Browning hastily added "The Pied Piper of Hamelin" the month before publication.[5] *Dramatic*

Lyrics thus has alternate endings. Far from marring the original design, Browning improvised brilliantly by placing at the end of the volume "The Pied Piper," with its comic focusing of the collection's increasing preoccupation with the role of the poet.

The arrangement of poems does not follow their chronology of composition. On the contrary, Browning wrote the opening "Cavalier Tunes" only a few months before publication, and he placed the earliest poems—"Madhouse Cells"—almost at the end.[6] The order instead follows a different principle, a thematic one, with formal considerations sometimes reinforcing the formation of the pairs. By consisting of three lyrics, the opening "Cavalier Tunes" stands apart from the pairs as much as the unpaired lyrics do. Far from merely antiquarian, "Cavalier Tunes" capitalizes on the intense interest in the English Civil Wars that swept the country in the bicentennial year 1842 and inaugurates the theme of loyalty and proper devotion on both the personal and political levels that dominates the ensuing volume. The first pair, "My Last Duchess" and "Count Gismond," contrasts the treatment of women in that regard within a frame which remains more personal than political and which calls attention to the acts of mind of the speakers. The second pair, "Camp and Cloister," suggests far more than the mere "pleasures of alliteration" to which one critic has limited it;[7] the self-sacrifice for love in "Incident of the French Camp" contrasts with the egocentric hatred of "Soliloquy of the Spanish Cloister," both set within the context of social institutions. Similarly, in the following implicit pair, "In a Gondola" presents the death of a lover in a true but illicit love, while "Artemis Prologuizes" presents the vengeful death of Hippolutos through the unrequited and illicit passion of his stepmother Phaedra. Standing by itself, "Waring" returns the volume to the social world of England in 1842, particularly the problem of emigration, and makes explicit the concern with poetry that will climax in the final poem. "Queen-Worship" then contrasts amorous devotion in a courtly and a contemporary context in which the modern seems almost tawdry by comparison. "Madhouse Cells" treats egoistic delusions about God and the moral law, with "Johannes Agricola in Meditation" offering a theological equivalent to the corruption of personal relations in "Porphyria's Lover." The original ending, "Through the Metidja to Abd-El-Kadr.—1842" returns the volume to the contemporary world, with an Arab horseman's devotion to his prince in a colonial war of independence balancing the opening treatment of Cavalier devotion at the start of the volume. The alternate ending, "The Pied Piper of Hamelin," ponders in comic guise the role of the poet in society, and of history or legend in contemporary life, that has increasingly preoccupied *Dramatic Lyrics*. The remainder of this essay explores the pertinence to each poem of its place in the overall scheme. Such analysis illuminates not only the neglected poems of the collection but also even those that have attracted copious individual commentary.

The title "Cavalier Tunes," like that of *Dramatic Lyrics* itself, diverts attention to the form and speaker of the poems, and encourages us to separate persona from poet. Stung by criticism of the personal nature of his earlier verse, Browning described the new poems in his 1842 "advertisement" as "often Lyric in expression, always Dramatic in principle, and so many utterances of so many imaginary persons, not mine" (p. 347). No one was likely to confuse the young poet with the bluff Royalist speaker of the tunes, particularly since his sympathies with the Parliamentarians had crept into *Strafford* five years before (they would surface again as late as the song for Pym at the end of "Parleying with Charles Avison," 1887). To animate such a speaker required an act of historical imagination. Capitalizing on the interest surrounding the 1842 bicentenary of the start of the English Civil War may have been another way of bolstering Browning's continually disappointed hopes for early popularity, which had prompted issuance of the *Dramatic Lyrics* number of *Bells and Pomegranates* in the first place.[8] But more important, "Cavalier Tunes" suggests the imaginative recovery of living history that Browning preferred to mere antiquarian or factual narrative, and that he practiced in the remainder of the volume as he had previously in *Sordello*. The tunes provided an accessible paradigm to a contemporary English reader of the strategies that shape the ensuing succession of medieval and Renaissance courts, Spanish cloister, French camp, Greek myth, madhouse cells, or exotic contemporary locales like Venice, Trieste, and Algeria.

The sequence of Cavalier poems both establishes an internal order and introduces the volume thematically. They pertain to three different stages of the Civil War, from the road to Nottingham where the war began in 1642 (in "Marching Along") through the intermediate phase of struggle (in "Give a Rouse") to the rejection of surrender (in "Boot and Saddle"). The fierce political loyalty of the Cavalier anticipates that of the French boy and Arab horseman later in the volume, and it contrasts with the emotions driving the envious monk, the gentle Waring, the lascivious Queen Cristina, or the duplicitous burghers of Hamelin. Similarly, the Cavalier enjoys the full support of a united family, including his son George and wife Gertrude. This family harmony contrasts, of course, with the intrigues of Ferrara, Aix, and Spain, the extramarital passion of contemporary Venice or ancient Greece, and the perverse emotions of Porphyria's lover; it finds an echo in the devotion of Count Gismond and of Rudel. The original title of "Boot and Saddle" in 1842, "My Wife Gertrude," emphasized the familial solidarity in particular preparation for the following pair of poems.

While the original titles of that pair, "Italy" and "France," emphasize place, the revised ones by which we now know them, "My Last Duchess" and "Count Gismond," stress character, with setting (Ferrara and Aix in Provence) relegated to subtitles. Initially, Browning obviously meant to contrast the forms of aristocratic attitudes toward marriage in patriarchal Italy and chivalric Provence. But the revised titles point attention to an aspect of the two poems that illuminates the rationale of their original pairing and later dispersal. The later titles call attention not just to character but to particular characters, the Duchess and the Count, both of whom are innocents. More important, they function analogously in their respective poems as stimuli to the mental action of the more complicated character who delivers each dramatic monologue. For all the thematic links—innocence versus corruption, wife as chattel versus wife as chivalric Lady, Italian society versus French, and the like—the link in mental action of the speaker binds the two poems together most tightly.

As he utters his discourse, the acts of mind of the Duke recapitulate those in a Greater Romantic Lyric, which Browning would adapt more subtly in "Pictor Ignotus" three years later. Briefly, as M. H. Abrams has argued, Greater Romantic Lyrics exhibit a three-part structure based on mental action rather than formal verse divisions; they present a definite speaker in a determinate landscape with which mind interacts first in a detached, then involved, then again detached way in a series that may be described as out-in-out or, as I argue in the following chapters, description-vision-evaluation. Displacements in time or space accompany the shifting psychological states, and the language often rises from vernacular to more formal speech.[9] Such poems always return to their opening scene at the end, and the middle section typically involves memory (as in Wordsworth) or imagination (as in Keats). Wordsworth's "Tintern Abbey" and "Elegiac Stanzas Suggested by a Picture of Peele Castle," Coleridge's "Eolian Harp" and other conversation poems, and Keats's "Ode on a Grecian Urn" and "Ode to a Nightingale" all exemplify the pattern. So, too, do "My Last Duchess" and "Pictor Ignotus," among other works of Browning, whose speaker—like Keats's contemplating the urn or Wordsworth's before Beaumont's painting—typically substitutes an artwork (here, the portrait of the Duchess) for a natural landscape.

In "My Last Duchess" a tripartite structure reenacts the romantic paradigm even while parodying it by denying the imaginative insight that the Romantics represented there. The Duke begins with present description of the painting and of his guest's alleged reaction to it. In the middle of line 13 ("Sir, 'twas not . . .") he shifts to past tense, in which memory recounts the Duchess's behavior until her death. Memory continues until the middle of line 46, when he breaks off its flow to return to the present tense and original scene ("There she stands") for a new purpose. The monologue thus presents a three-part progression based on acts of mind (description-memory-description/evaluation) supported by displacements in time (now-then-now) and place (in front of the portrait—elsewhere in the palace and grounds—in front of the portrait again). But while earlier Greater Romantic Lyrics typically climax the intense second section at a moment of imaginative intensity, like Keats imagining a town not on the urn or the perilous seas of fairyland, the Duke builds toward an act of murder that represents the opposite of imaginative sympathy before his return to the present scene. Wrapped in his egotism, he remains wholly within himself even as his discourse follows a form originally designed to show annihilation of selfhood through imagination. Like the other villains of the volume, the alpha and omega of his discourse are "that's my" and "for me!" in contrast to the devotion to others shown by the positive figures. A perverse desire to possess the moment reduces a living person to a dead object both literally and figuratively, as Browning emphasizes later in the collection (most markedly in "Porphyria's Lover") and elsewhere.

Similar formal and thematic patterns underlie the superficially different companion poem, "Count Gismond," which displays both an overt contrast and a covert kinship to "My Last Duchess." The contrast, of course, concerns the treatment of women, while the kinship involves the revelation of egoistic manipulation of others through a particular form of discourse. Without joining the revisionist ranks intent on supporting the 1842 pairing by turning the Countess into a counterpart of the depraved Duke, I do think that the more solid arguments for that position compel a reading that at least holds open the possibility of her duplicity. Chief among them are the predatory emphasis of the falcon imagery, the preoccupation with details like the dripping sword, the distinction in appearance of the two boys, and the fact that the Countess does conclude with a lie intended to deceive Gismond, whether tactfully caring or symptomatically corrupt. [10]

The parallels between the Countess's discourse and the Duke's reinforce a subversive reading. Here Browning's revisions in the titles help, for each emphasizes a character, the Duchess and the Count, who resemble each other and play analogous roles in their respective poems. They are innocents, and they inspire the monologues of their more complicated spouses. Like the Duke, the Countess begins in the present with her prayer for the Count's salvation, moves into the past through memory for the bulk of her utterance, and returns to the present at the end ("Gismond here?"). The one break in the central section, a fleeting return to the present in lines 49–50, both follows romantic precedent in poems like "Tintern Abbey" and calls attention to the content of that interruption, a concern that Gismond not hear her. Further, like the Duke, the Countess favors first-person pronouns at revealing times; at the beginning she wants God to save Gismond because he "saved me," and at the end she accepts his bringing "my" tercel back, while her whole middle account focuses on her changing status and situation. The Countess may or may not equal the Duke in depravity, but she does resemble him in an egotism that sees others only as means to her own ends and that forswears the potential for imaginative self-transcendence in the acts of mind that structure her account.

The ensuing 1842 pairing, "Camp and Cloister," extends the contrast between egoistic hatred and self-sacrifice for love from marriage to two other social institutions, the army and religion. The two poems thus contrast with each other thematically even as they continue the larger dichotomy between virtuous and vicious characters that the volume repeatedly presents. In form, too, the overt correspondence of their eight-line stanzas composed of alternately rhyming quatrains yields to a deeper contrast by which the straightforward narrative of the boy's heroism serves as foil to the circuitous associations of the monk's rancor. When Browning retitled the poems for 1849, he again de-emphasized geography, this time stressing character in action rather than the action in character of "My Last Duchess" and "Count Gismond." As title, "Incident of the French Camp" highlights the event as much as the locale, while "Soliloquy of the Spanish Cloister" suggests an ensuing action to follow the self-revelation of soliloquy.

The poems themselves belie the stock expectations of their own titles, with the armed camp, associated with martial violence, here featuring loving devotion and the cloister, associated with contemplative quiet, here full of sound and fury. The characters both contrast with each other and establish a series of links to other figures in the collection. The French boy, like the Italian Duchess and the French Count Gismond, displays the virtue of innocence in his selfless devotion to the emperor. But Napoleon differs from the Duke in responding sympathetically to such traits. Similarly, the use of predatory bird imagery contrasts with the Countess's fondness for fighting falcons; at sight of the boy's wound, the emperor's eye softens "as sheathes / A film the mother-eagle's eye / When her bruised eaglet breathes." Just as the devoted boy's happiness in death anticipates that of the lover of "In a Gondola" and of Rudel, so has the exasperated reaction of vice to virtue in "My Last Duchess" prefigured that of the monk to Friar Lawrence in "Soliloquy of the Spanish Cloister." Lawrence obviously belongs with the boy and the Duchess, while the speaker belongs with the Duke and, later in the volume, Porphyria's lover. The interruptions, tags of conversation, and disturbed rhythms that give the poem its modernity all betoken the monk's derangement at the sight of a virtue that he remakes into a projection of his own vices. He is a powerless Duke, who would kill Lawrence if he could. Just as his empty formalism recalls the Duke's preoccupation with protocol, so does the monk's monologue begin and end with a keynote—in his case the animalistic "Gr-r-r" that reduces him from the human to the bestial level even as he brands his enemy a "swine." Both this poem and its companion play central roles in the evolving unity of the volume as a whole.

Unlike the previous groupings, "In a Gondola" and "Artemis Prologuizes" do not share a common title, but they do form an implicit pair in which a male lover meets his death through illicit passion. They thus continue the troubled relationships between men and women that preoccupy the volume. As a diptych they display a series of contrasts that rival those of Browning's other pairings of poems with related themes. The Venetian lover of "In a Gondola" dies of his own reciprocated passion for a married woman, whereas the Greek Hippolutos dies because of his refusal to share the adulterous love of his infatuated stepmother. Both poems present an intense moment with catastrophic aftereffects, in one a moment of love and the other of lust for revenge. The Venetian woman seems to rejoice in the death of her lover at the height of his passion (as he himself does), whereas Artemis strives to resuscitate her votary. Formally, the dialogue of the first poem allows it to contrast the attitudes of the two lovers themselves, while the second depends upon the retrospective omniscience of Artemis. Perhaps most important for overall design, "In a Gondola" presents actual human speakers placed in a contemporary if distant city, while "Artemis Prologuizes" avows frankly its mythological status. Although earlier in the volume "Cavalier Tunes" recalls the bicentenary of the Civil Wars, "Incident of the French Camp" may remember the impressive second burial of Napoleon in December of 1841, and even "Soliloquy of the Spanish Cloister" may glance at the debate over religious ritual stirred by the Oxford Movement, "Artemis Prologuizes" stands at the farthest remove from Victorian England of any poem in the volume. Browning has followed his recurrent themes into a mythic dimension, but he has also left the contemporary world behind.

He returns to that world abruptly and ambivalently in "Waring." Placed in the middle of the volume, immediately after the escape from history into Greek mythology, "Waring" redirects the reader's attention to contemporary England. The poem not only draws on the general interest of the increased emigration from England to the colonies that would continue to swell as the Hungry Forties progressed, but also has a particular model in Browning's friend Alfred Domett, who had just departed for New Zealand.[11] Further, the poem itself assumes a chatty topicality as it progresses through the conditions of early Victorian art, literature, and society. Its colloquial tone, by turns mock-heroic, bantering, and lyrical, reinforces the contrast to "Artemis Prologuizes," with its stately blank verse. Calling attention to itself by being unpaired in a volume of pairs, "Waring" arrests the historical and mythic movement of the volume.

Waring himself evokes an ambivalent response. On the one hand, the tone clearly is sympathetic toward him: The speaker misses Waring, believes in his promise, and implores him to return and "Bring the

real times back, confessed / Still better than our very best!" On the
other hand, the speaker gently mocks his friend "With no work done, /
But great works undone," addresses him in a mock-heroic, biblical
lament ("Ichabod, Ichabod, / The glory is Departed!"), and betrays a
recurrent skepticism about Waring's ability to translate his powers into
achievement. For Waring himself has forsaken the England to which
the poem calls so much attention, even in the fantasy of his possible,
secret return. Like Arnold's scholar-gypsy, whom he resembles in
cultivation, gentleness, and flight from Victorian England, Waring
turns out to be an insufficient artist-figure to redeem modern malaise.[12]
The glimpse of Waring on the Trieste boat at the end of the poem
mirrors the glimpse of the scholar-gypsy in the English countryside.
Both poems require a sterner figure as alternative to contemporary ills.
"The Scholar-Gypsy" ends with the alternate vision of the Tyrian
trader; Browning's poem ends only with Waring, but the volume itself
will conclude first with the fierce image of the Arab horseman and then
with the Piper, still outside society but more effective in his art than the
gentle exile of "Waring."

   Between "Waring" and the concluding poems, Browning placed two
more pairs, "Queen-Worship" and "Madhouse Cells." Comprising
"Rudel and the Lady of Tripoli" and "Cristina," "Queen-Worship"
presents a diptych of male devotion to contrasting female beloveds.
The first poem contains two direct links to "Waring": First, like War-
ing, Rudel is a poet; and second, just as "Waring" urges us to "Look
East" (line 261), so does Rudel in the last line look "to the East—the
East!" Among the many revisions, the change of "and" to "to" in the
title focuses attention all the more on Rudel, the Troubadour poet-
lover. According to legend, he fell in love with the Princess of Tripoli
by hearing pilgrims' accounts of her beauty, wrote several poems of
chaste but hopeless love for her, eventually sailed to Tripoli, and died
in her arms. The story presents a typical tale of a Troubadour's chiv-
alrous devotion to the beauty of his married lady, who herself behaves
with perfect circumspection. In contrast, Browning selected as the lady
for the modern poem of the pair the licentious Maria Cristina of Spain.
Cristina, the young fourth wife of Ferdinand VII, acted as Queen until
his death in 1833 and then as regent for her daughter until 1840, when
revelation of her secret marriage to the soldier Muñoz forced her to
abdicate. Throughout her career she earned a reputation as a notorious
coquette.[13] Her promiscuity thus opposes the Lady of Tripoli's virtue.

Yet the male lover of "Cristina" expresses devotion to her in an avowal of a "moment" when their "souls rushed together" that accords with Browning's sympathy elsewhere for the doctrine of Elective Affinities.[14] Without the title, such doctrines could be taken at face value here, too. But the title ascribes the affinities to such a ludicrously inappropriate figure that it calls into question the stability of the speaker. He creates a fantasy world for himself that has little relation to the actual one surrounding him. In that way, he prepares us for the more exaggerated pathology of the next two speakers, Johannes Agricola and Porphyria's lover.

Browning chose for the final pair in the volume the two he had written and published first. The placement does not derive from an attempt to bury early works of poor quality; except for "My Last Duchess" and "Soliloquy of the Spanish Cloister," the poems now known as "Johannes Agricola in Meditation" and "Porphyria's Lover" can stand with any in the collection, as their frequent inclusion in anthologies suggests. Rather, the poems serve as thematic culmination to the collection. A clue to this lies in their joint title, "Madhouse Cells," which Browning devised for the 1842 volume (it was not part of their first appearance, in Fox's *Monthly Repository* for January 1836), kept for the 1849 *Dramatic Romances and Lyrics* when he reprinted the poems of 1842 and 1845 in their original order, and dropped when he broke the pairing as part of the general rearrangement of 1863. Through the title Browning controls our responses more obtrusively than he has heretofore done. "Madhouse Cells" brands the speakers as unreliable, even deranged, from the start. Yet it only makes explicit what other poems have left implicit. All of Browning's villainous speakers figuratively inhabit cells betokening isolation and social deviance, ringed round with self-delusion. The Duke, Countess Gismond (in the more negative interpretation of her), and the Spanish monk, for example, betray the same traits as Browning's madhouse speakers: They hold themselves exempt from laws that bind others, confuse empty formalism with moral legitimacy, and see others only as projections of their own psychic needs. In contrast, positive figures like the Cavalier, French boy, Rudel, and Arab horseman accept their social obligations, place spirit above letter, and serve others.

While the two poems overlap, "Johannes Agricola" stresses exemption from the laws that bind others, "Porphyria's Lover" the treatment of a lover as an object which corrupts the male-female relations of the volume. Browning allots each view equal space: Both poems contain exactly sixty lines of iambic tetrameter rhymed *a b a b b* in the most exact parallelism of any of the pairs. The historical Johannes Agricola (1494–1566) at first supported Luther but then broke with him to help found Antinomianism, a doctrine that Browning summarized in the 1836 printing by a headnote taken from Defoe's *Dictionary of All Religions*:

> Antinomians, so denominated for rejecting the Law as a thing of no use under the Gospel dispensation: they say, that good works do not further, nor evil works hinder salvation; that the child of God cannot sin, that God never chastiseth him, *that murder, drunkenness, &c. are sins in the wicked but not in him,* that the child of grace being once assured of salvation, afterwards never doubteth . . . that God doth not love any man for his holiness, that sanctification is no evidence of justification, &c. Pontanus, in his Catalogue of Heresies, says John Agricola was the author of this sect, A.D. 1535.[15] (italics mine)

The whole volume, as well as Browning's positions elsewhere, rejects such a view. The suppression of Johannes's name from the title for only the 1842 text reinforces the general applicability of the poem by removing the possibility of historical restriction. Like the villains of *Dramatic Lyrics*, Johannes combines his exemption from laws that bind others with excessive reliance on the first-person pronoun in inappropriate contexts: His first ten lines emphasize "I" and the next twenty "me," as though God had designed the cosmos expressly for Johannes Agricola or, as he says, "for me."

"Porphyria's Lover" extends Johannes's doctrines to the personal realm, with disastrous results. Like "My Last Duchess," "Count Gismond," and "Artemis Prologuizes," the poem presents a murder between the sexes as both the literal and figurative result of treating the beloved as an object. And like the Duke, Porphyria's lover seems unable to distinguish an inanimate object, whether portrait or corpse, from the living person. In place of the Duke's abortion of the Greater Romantic Lyric pattern in a failure of imaginative sympathy, the lover here lapses into a syntactic pattern of ands that seem to connect his narrative syntactically and yet rob it of true connection by placing all events, including the murder, on the same syntactic level. The result is a freezing of mental action, which imprisons the lover in his own mind as surely as he is imprisoned in his madhouse cell. Whatever the flirtatiousness of Porphyria herself, her lover is no lover at all. Neither are any of the other villains of the volume, whereas the heroes and heroines display the ability to love so central to Browning's later work.

Following the thematic climax of "Madhouse Cells," the volume reaches its original conclusion with "Through the Metidja to Abd-El-Kadr.—1842." This poem gives the collection a circular shape by returning to the situation of the opening lyric and, like all the unpaired poems, tying it to the historical present. A popular hero of the day, the sultan and emir Abd-El-Kadr waged a war of resistance against the French after their conquest of Algeria in 1830. After initial successes, including occupation of the Metidja or great plain of Algiers, he encountered increased French pressure under Marshal Bugeaud from 1842 onwards and finally surrendered in 1847. The Algerian's attempt to rally the tribes behind him was reported in *The Times* throughout June of 1842, at about the time of the poem's composition.[16] Like the bicentenary of the Civil Wars and the emigration of which Domett was a part, then, the events of the poem return the reader to political news in contemporary England. The poem also would have concluded the volume fitly. Like "Cavalier Tunes," it presents a horseman riding to the support of his beleaguered prince. Like the portraits of positive figures and unlike those of the villains, it presents a character devoted to a cause or person outside of himself. The Arab horseman's "full heart" combines allegiance to Abd-El-Kadr with satisfaction and pride in that service. Equally importantly for Browning, the horseman is a figure of activity, striving to realize his ideals in the world rather than to rationalize them. He represents character in action.

When the publisher Edward Moxon informed Browning that the poems he originally submitted for *Dramatic Lyrics* did not fill the projected sixteen-page format, Browning responded by sending him the recently completed "Pied Piper of Hamelin."[17] Far from spoiling the design of the volume, this improvisation preserved its integrity while refocusing its major preoccupations. Admittedly, Browning subtitled the poem "A Child's Story" written for William Macready the Younger, son of the great tragedian. Yet within its comic plot and occasionally doggerel verse, "The Pied Piper" offers a humorous meditation on the role of the artist in society that had begun in the volume with "Waring." Indeed, the two poems were written nearly at the same time, together with the essay on Chatterton. [18] All three works worried a great deal over the character of the unappreciated and perhaps ineffectual artist within a mercantile society. The poem itself presents the piper as an artist-figure. To begin with, he is a piper, a traditional image of the poet. His clothes and appearance distinguish him from others, in a manner familiar at least since Werther and Byron. His fingers are never far from his pipe. He possesses "a secret charm" for affecting others (line 72) and makes "wonderful music" (line 207). Most important of all, like much postromantic poetry his music offers visions of paradise to its audience. This paradise assumes an appropri-ately mock-epic form in the apples, conserves, and butter-casks of the rats and a more lyrical and pastoral one in the "joyous land" (line 240) of fruit-trees, gushing water, and "strange and new" creatures that attract the children. When the burghers break their promise to reward the piper, his art turns from beneficent to demonic in its effects. [19]

Besides its stress on the role of the poet, "The Pied Piper" picks up three other themes from the volume. First, it professes a double status both as an historical account and as a legendary one. Browning care-fully begins by fixing the location of the town of Hamelin and establish-ing the date of the ensuing events as "Almost five hundred years ago." As always, his treatment is neither antiquarian nor annalistic but rather concerned to revivify events for the present in a way that stresses their contemporary application. Second, the burghers of Hamelin belong with the company from the Duke onward who seek to use others only for their own ends and to exempt themselves from normal social obligations. They have promised him a thousand guilders for his perfor-mance but renege upon their pledge as soon as he has provided his service. And third, like the other unpaired poems this one has special relevance to England in 1842. For in that year a new Literary Copyright Act was passed after long advocacy by Macaulay and petitions to the House of Commons by Carlyle among others. [20] The issue of payment to the artist, and the implications of that payment as an index of his relation to bourgeois society, troubled not just fourteenth-century Hamelin but also nineteenth-century England. It troubled as well Robert Browning, whose works had never sold well and whose new effort at reaching a wider public in *Dramatic Lyrics* was to suffer the customary disappointment of those years. Yet in *Dramatic Lyrics* Brow-ning had not only concluded major dramatic monologues of the sort that would eventually cement his reputation, but he had also artfully arranged them into an overall design that deepened the significance of each individual part. Just as inclusion of "The Pied Piper" in the volume increases the pertinence of its ironic presentation of the poet's role, so do the various pairs highlight contrasts and continuities within each diptych and among the groupings themselves. "Cavalier Tunes" and "Through the Metidja" enrich each other. So, too, does the Duke's manipulative egotism interact with the account of the Countess, or the chivalric devotion of Rudel rhyme with the skewed dedication of Porphyria's lover. His audience is still learning to read Robert Browning.

3 The Structure of Browning's "Pictor Ignotus"

I f Browning's "Pictor Ignotus" has not itself become a poema ignotum of modern scholarship, it has at least been unduly neglected. Relegated to the shadows of two perhaps greater monologues spoken by painters, "Fra Lippo Lippi" and "Andrea del Sarto," the poem has escaped from mention in passing chiefly to inspire either correction of DeVane's early and influential sympathy for the speaker or strained identification of the unknown pictor with a known painter, usually Fra Bartolommeo.[1] Yet "Pictor Ignotus" deserves better. Its intricacies of structure make it one of the most finely crafted of the dramatic monologues and reveal Browning's creative transformation of romantic norms in the ongoing development of nineteenth-century poetry. To see that, we need to think of structure not as an array of formal devices, still less as an organizing principle separate from content, but rather as an arrangement of sequential acts of mind by the speaker which comprise at once both the form and the content of the poem. The pictor's discourse both describes and reenacts his abortive career. In this essay I mean to analyze the pattern of mental action in "Pictor Ignotus" within a frame situating Browning's dramatic monologue as a postromantic development.

The increasingly frequent emphasis on acts of mind in discussions of postromantic poetry[2] accords well with Browning's own theory and practice. For example, he announced in the 1835 introduction to *Paracelsus* his intention

> to reverse the method usually adopted by writers whose aim
> it is to set forth any phenomenon of the mind or the pas-

sions, by the operation of persons and events; and that, instead of having recourse to an external machinery of incidents to create and evolve the crisis I desire to produce, I have ventured *to display somewhat minutely the mood itself in its rise and progress,* and have suffered the agency by which it is influenced and determined, to be generally discernible in its effects alone, and subordinate throughout, if not altogether excluded: and this for a reason. I have endeavoured to write a poem, not a drama.[3] (italics mine)

"Mood" in the italicized phrase presumably incorporates phenomena of both "the mind" and "the passions" mentioned earlier. Displaying its "rise and progress" commits Browning to a poetry in which mental actions form an ordered sequence. He avowed a similar intent two years later, when he described *Strafford* as representing "Action in Character rather than Character in Action" (II, 9). The action which takes place in character is, of course, mental, as opposed to the physical display of character in action. Yet neither *Paracelsus* nor *Strafford* chooses the proper vehicle for such display. Like the monodrama which it resembles,[4] *Paracelsus* makes the "mood" sometimes too general and sometimes too independent from the speaker. Correspondingly, the stage drama *Strafford* neglects many resources of the theater in focusing on a kind of action difficult to display there. But the dramatic monologue, with which he had already begun to experiment, offered Browning the ideal vehicle to combine the action in character of *Strafford* with the progress of the mood itself in *Paracelsus.*

We can best study mental action in monologues like "Pictor Ignotus" by continuing to think of them as (in Robert Langbaum's justly influential phrase) a "poetry of experience" but resisting the tendency to explore the tension between sympathy and judgment in their effect—in short, to emphasize the speaker's experience as he utters the poem over the reader's reaction as he hears it. The closest paradigm for the experience of "Pictor Ignotus" lies in the genre of the Greater Romantic Lyric, which the previous chapter applied to "My Last Duchess." Usually, such a poem attains a tripartite structure by returning upon itself to end with the original scene, most frequently a landscape but sometimes an artwork instead, as in "Ode on a Grecian Urn." The distinctive contribution of "Pictor Ignotus" lies superficially in substituting an indoor and artistic setting for landscape and more deeply in tracing its action so "minutely" that it offers transitional sections into and out of the vision proper.

The acts of mind which comprise the "Action in Character" or "mood itself in its rise and progress" of "Pictor Ignotus" (IV, 164–66) occupy five distinct stages which correspond to quatrain divisions. In the first three quatrains (ll. 1–12) the speaker describes his present situation and rationalizes his rival's success and his own comparative failure. In the next three quatrains (ll. 13–24) he advances a series of personifications (Hope, Rapture, and Confidence) which, despite some lameness, shift his discourse toward a more imaginative level. The three succeeding sections of four quatrains each depict first a glimpse of that level and then its devastating aftermath. Lines 25–40 present the most imaginative section of the poem, a vision of fame and friendship cast as an account of a dream. Lines 41–56 break off the vision at its most intense moment and dissolve into associative recoil which both expresses the speaker's fear and reenacts his inability to sustain the dream. The final section, lines 57–72, returns to the level of conversational language in which the speaker concludes his self-justification. A key word here is the "Wherefore" which begins line 57. In terms of argumentative content, "wherefore" signals the concluding stage in the pictor's rationalizing argument.[5] But in terms of mental action, "wherefore" concludes his reenactment of his failure to sustain his own vision. For just as in his career the pictor abandoned his early imaginative vision for the "monotonous" (l. 58) reproduction of a received iconography, so does his very account of his career rise to the imaginative level and then abandon it, to end in the comforting rationalizations of discursive language. Let us examine more carefully Browning's skillful arrangement of each successive stage.

Pictor begins the first section of the poem (ll. 1–12) in medias res with a remark couched in everyday diction expressing an ordinary, discursive frame of mind which contrasts even with the remainder of this section: "I could have painted pictures like that youth's / Ye praise so." The ensuing trite metaphor of the soul springing up triggers the more vital and elevated sentence which follows, as though in recollecting that time the speaker's soul does again spring up. His speech embodies the very vigor it recalls. The headlong rhythm and vivid verbs ("outburst," "shrunk," "sunk") match the splendid metaphor of the painter outbursting on the night like stars and the soul rising to heaven or sinking to the center. The turbulent verticality of those images recalls the pervasive up-and-down movement of Shelley's verse (whether the flight of the skylark or the continual rising and falling in *Prometheus Unbound*), just as the lines themselves fit Browning's description of the subjective poet in his essay on Shelley.[6] They contrast with the slower, more balanced, but still formal lines which complete the section and render the objective poet, whose eye turns to man rather than to divine Ideas. Yet even these lines register the gain in poise and power: "Allowed to truth made visible in man" suggests a prophetic scope far removed from the querulous opening line.

Yet for all the development in the initial section, the discourse displays omens of the abortive rather than triumphant mental action to come. First, and most obviously, negatives control the syntax in the long and otherwise energetic third sentence: "No" (l. 2), "Never" (l. 4), and "nor" (l. 6). They dissociate the speaker from the positive energy of his expression and forebode his failure to harness his own powers. Second, the pictor fails to understand his own mental processes. He observes that thought of the absence of external restraint "saddens while it soothes" when in the poem it does just the opposite: It excites rather than soothes him and (to judge by the vigor of the rest of the sentence) elates rather than saddens. A third signal was clearer in the original 1845 text of lines 6–7, where Browning wrote "this flesh" and "that soul" instead of the 1849 "my flesh" and "my soul." The deleted demonstrative adjectives seem further to doom the speaker by implying that, although he occupies the same body, he now lacks the soul which enabled him once to soar or sink so grandly. But even without this third clue the speaker's acts of mind in the opening section still foreshadow the eventual misfire of his discourse.

The progress begun in the shift from ordinary to more charged language continues through the two mental actions of the second part (ll. 13–24)—the unification of opposites and the envisioning of personifications. Repetition of the phrase "that youth ye praise so" in line 13 returns the painter to his starting point in diction but not in mental power, for he has entered a different psychological stage. The rest of that sentence embodies a series of overt and implicit opposites, fulfilling Coleridge's claim that imagination manifests itself in a balance or reconciliation of opposite or discordant qualities. Besides the antinomial quality of "Each passion clear proclaimed without a tongue" and the implicit oxymoron of "passion's law," the passage turns on the opposing connotation of "flung" at the end of line 14 (wildness, escape from restraint) and "law" at the end of line 15 (order, discipline). The speaker's ability to combine such opposites testifies to his growing imaginative power at this point in his monologue, just as his later inability to fuse the opposites of the concluding lines will signal his imaginative exhaustion. He next launches into a series of personifications in two-line vignettes of Hope rising tiptoe, Rapture drooping her eyes, and Confidence lighting the forehead and locking the mouth. In an influential note Philip Drew has characterized these as "laboured personifications,"[7] but I think that their slight heaviness functions only secondarily, as a further warning of the limits of the painter's powers as speaker. Primarily, they represent a growing imaginative force which discharges itself in the creation of these imaginary vignettes before reaching its climax in the vision of triumphant success that constitutes part three. Further, Browning has not picked these personifications at random: Hope, Rapture, and Confidence are the precise qualities the pictor lacks. They function ironically for the reader, reinforcing the disparity between his and the speaker's knowledge. For the speaker, though, they again signify an accession of mental power through memory of his own repudiated aims. It is as though in the act of recollecting them he temporarily reassumes the very qualities he has denied.

Before progressing to his strongest vision the pictor momentarily relapses. The lines "O human faces, hath it spilt, my cup? / What did ye give me that I have not saved?" (ll. 23–24) adumbrate the inability of the speaker to maintain his imaginative commitment in the face of the human distraction or detraction which dominates the fourth section of the poem. Again, the 1845 text rendered the disparity more sharply, with its more detailed, "Men, women, children" instead of the generalized "human faces." Commentators usually gloss the obvious biblical allusion of those lines in terms of the overflowing cup, but I suggest that the parable of the steward who buried his talent in the ground (Matthew 25) is even more pertinent. Like his biblical predecessor who by burying his talent (as coin) in the ground preserved but failed to increase it, the pictor kept the talent (as ability) he was given but failed to make it flourish. Though he has been given nothing he has not saved, he has still proved a false steward.

The growing power in both the pictor's career and his acts of mind climaxes in the vision of lines 25–40. The long sentence recounting the triumphant progress of the imaginary picture reenacts the very dream it relates. The speaker begins on a general and public level but grows more specific as he goes along, as though he becomes caught up in the details of his own account. The generalized enumeration of possible patrons, directions, and destinations (in 1845 universalized rather than generalized through use of "and" instead of the later "or") yields to the concrete details of the flowers cast upon the car and the arrival of the car at the speaker's "home" (in 1845 even more specific through the pronoun "my"). The steady increase in reality for the speaker of what started out as memory of a dream culminates in the shift in tense of lines 33–35, where the subjunctive "should greet" replaces the previous past tense and then suppression of the "should" in "lie learning at my feet" creates an effect of immediacy, as though the scene actually were taking place. At this point the speaker has been caught up in his own vision, and he exclaims the four rapturous lines that follow, in which he imagines the protracted bliss of love and fame.

If in the act of telling his dream of creating a masterpiece the speaker takes on momentarily the very power of imagination which producing such an artwork would demand, the opening and closing lines which frame that act indicate why he never succeeded. Pictor fears his own powers of imagination. Thus, he begins the vision with a double negative rather than with a positive assertion: "Nor will I say I have not dreamed." The awkward construction functions less as polite self-deprecation to disarm a listener than as a means of the speaker's defending against the imaginative force of the ensuing utterance by distancing himself from it. As Herbert Tucker has aptly pointed out, "In the original edition of 1845, Browning put line 40 into the present tense as a reminder that the Pictor is still engaged in repressing present possibilities."[8] Even in revised form that concluding line of the vision makes the fear explicit: "The thought grew frightful, 'twas so wildly dear!" "Frightful" and "wildly," like "scared me" two lines later, suggest an intensity and freedom which render the speaker's own imaginative power alarming to him. In that, as in his baffled retreat into repetitive custom, he resembles a later speaker like Prufrock in T. S. Eliot's dramatic monologues.

Recoil from vision into a sort of associative derangement occupies the four quatrains of the following section. Although the reasons offered here for the failure of his career seem to be rationalizations, the mode of mental action in these quatrains recapitulates the retreat from imagination into distraught association which caused the failure. Significantly, he starts trains of imagery which he can only break off rather than conclude, just as in life he broke off his dream rather than execute the picture that would accomplish it. First comes the comparison to rites of idolatry and then, signalled by the syntactic lapse of the ellipsis in line 46, the uncompleted analogy to soldiers raping a nun. The fear driving both of these figures of speech causes the speaker to interrupt them before completion, and to retreat into the pose of contempt for his audience which comprises the rest of the section. Only with re-establishment of that pose does the agitated dissociation of this transitional passage subside into relative restraint and control.

The content of the two similes extends the fear mimed by the mental action. The first applies to such "sights" as, presumably, the immediately preceding vision of the picture in public triumph which so disconcert the speaker that he can refer only to "Glimpses of such sights" rather than to the sights themselves. They "scared me, like the revels through a door / Of some strange house of idols at its rites!" Here not just the paganism or heresy of idolatry scares him, but particularly the release in "revels" of its devotees. Likewise, the simile of his stooping and shrinking from viewers "as from the soldiery a nun" again leads to the frenzy of the attempted rape. The violence and fear haunting both similes in this dissociative section contrast with the exaltation of the previous vision. And yet each figure is the obverse of the other, for in the first he dominates others and in the second others dominate him. The pictor cannot conceive a mutually reciprocal love but only the victory of egotism (the others in his dream love him, not he them) or its obliteration (as in a rape). Neither can he conceive integrating the two faculties upon which the alternatives depend: Faced with the choice of pure imagination or its rejection, he chooses rejection.

With that act comes restoration of the everyday acts of mind which began the poem and which convict the speaker as surely as do the obvious rationalizations of their overt content. He admits as much in confessing that "My heart sinks, as monotonous I paint." Not only his art but also his mental faculties sink. Description and reason (not in its Wordsworthian most exalted mood but in its lower, rationalizing form) replace vision and imagination as he claims a hollow integrity and absence of censure in place of the lost glory. Similarly, the more orthodox syntax signals restoration of control at the expense of imaginative risk. The decline registers forcibly in the dissolution of opposites in the concluding rhetorical questions of the poem. Whereas earlier in the poem growing mental power had unified the opposites of tongueless speaking, passion's law, and ordered flinging, here the declining mental power separates praise and worth, harshness and the golden cry, and sweetness and the specks of earth by that false secondary power which multiplies distinctions. The acts of mind of the pictor's discourse recapitulate those of his career, and indicate why he now produces derivative pictures of Virgin, Babe, and Saint rather than original and imaginative ones.

The contrast of states of mind coalesces in the rendering of the two kinds of pictures in the poem, the sort he could have painted in the vision section and the kind he actually does produce in the final section. The actual pictures he describes differ point by point from the potential one he imagines. The "same series" offers obscurity and coldness in place of praise and love, exists in confined (the cloister) rather than open space (the triumphant progress), remains private rather than public, and is described in terms more aural (ll. 64–68) than visual. Most important, the imagined picture would "live" and offer him the means to live, whereas the actual ones can only "die" and allow him to do the same. Pictor's repudiation of imaginative power results in a new articulation of the universe of death which the Romantics feared. Like the common precursor of them all, Browning cannot praise a fugitive and cloistered virtue.

In exploring the mental action of "Pictor Ignotus," I have intended not to give a line-by-line explication of the poem but rather to indicate its intricate psychological structure in a manner which substantiates its claims to a high place among the products of Browning's postromantic artistry. The reenactment of the pictor's career in the acts of mind of the very discourse in which he recounts it offers a way of uniting form and content in this monologue. I believe that the same approach can be applied to the entire range of Browning's monologues, from the early associative juxtapositions of "Porphyria's Lover" through the three-part structure of the Duke's discourse to the final approach to Greater Romantic Lyric in "Abt Vogler." We have had fine studies of Browning's characters in these poems, of the characteristics of their form, and of the character of the reader's response. By paying attention to the acts of mind which both form and inform his monologues, we can unite their various aspects into a fuller appreciation of what Browning meant by "Action in Character" and why he chose this form to display it.

4 Solomon's Architectonics: The Greater Victorian Lyric

R obert Browning carefully began one of his closest ap-
proaches to Greater Romantic Lyric, "Abt Vogler," by
having his persona seated at the organ wish for the power of King
Solomon to build imposing structures. That power derives from lan-
guage, or what the poem conditionally calls the ability to "name the
ineffable name."[1] Against that hopeful linguistic project, we may set a
more futile and familiar biblical passage ascribed to King Solomon, "Of
making many books there is no end, and much study is a weariness of
the flesh." Both Browning and the Bible see Solomon as a great builder.
His architectural labor inevitably suggests that of the poet. In troping
poetry as a kind of temple associated with the great shrine in Jerusalem,
Browning follows a central line of English imagery, which we can see in
George Herbert's choosing the title *The Temple* for his poems or in
these lines from Dryden's "To My Dear Friend Mr. Congreve" (1694):

> Our age was cultivated thus at length;
> But what we gain'd in skill we lost in strength.
> Our Builders were, with want of Genius, curst;
> The second Temple was not like the first.[2]

The destruction of Solomon's original temple and the subsequent
efforts to rebuild it render the temple trope particularly appropriate to
the history of poetic forms, in which later builders appropriate the
original structure even while recognizing that its contemporary incar-
nation cannot—indeed must not—be like the first. Worrying about

Shakespeare as a model for contemporary Victorian poets, Matthew Arnold chose an architectural analogy from Goethe: "what distinguishes the artist from the mere amateur, says Goethe, is *Architectonicè* in the highest sense; that power of execution, which creates, forms, and constitutes: not the profoundness of single thoughts, not the richness of imagery, not the abundance of illustration."[3] Here I would like to apply the temple trope to the refashioning of Greater Romantic Lyric during the Victorian period in Arnold's architectonic sense.

My earlier discussions of "My Last Duchess" and "Pictor Ignotus" followed M. H. Abrams in defining the Greater Romantic Lyric as a descriptive-meditative poem in which a determinate speaker in a particularized setting carries on a sustained colloquy with himself, with the scene, or with a silent auditor, often rising from vernacular to more formal speech.[4] Abrams schematized the repeated three-part process in which the mind interacts with the setting and their interplay constitutes the poem as "out-in-out," to throw emphasis on the mind's relation to nature. I find it useful to modify Abrams's schema by thinking of the out-in-out process as one of description-vision-evaluation, to throw emphasis on the act of the mind in uttering the poem. Usually, displacements in time (now-then-now) and space (here-there-here) reinforce the central psychological displacement of the vision section. The first poem in the new genre was Coleridge's "The Eolian Harp," and many of his conversation poems—like "This Lime-Tree Bower My Prison" or "Frost at Midnight"—fit the pattern, sometimes with variations (the most prevalent being a fourth and final movement back "in"). So, too, do Wordsworth's "Tintern Abbey" and Keats's "Ode to a Nightingale" or (with the substitution of an artwork for a natural setting) "Ode on a Grecian Urn." Because of the tension between visionary and ordinary experience, such poems always contain a potential for self-division, which the Romantics tend to mitigate and the Victorians to exacerbate.

All three of the major Victorian poets adapted the Greater Romantic Lyric to their own uses. They employed the form sparingly but memorably—Tennyson in *In Memoriam* 95, Arnold in "Dover Beach" and "The Scholar-Gypsy," and Browning in numerous monologues running from "My Last Duchess" through "Pictor Ignotus" to "Abt Vogler." Like Greater Romantic Lyrics, those poems feature a tripartite structure with a determinate speaker in a particularized setting; for Browning, as for Keats in front of the Urn, that setting more often features an artwork than a landscape. Yet despite such similarities in structure and style, the Victorian temple was not like the first. Tennyson, Arnold, and Browning introduced enough changes into the basic plan to warrant the postulation of a Greater Victorian Lyric as a subset of the broader form. Most simply, the Greater Victorian Lyric differs from its predecessor in two main and related ways. First, the Victorian poems display an even greater linguistic self-consciousness than the romantic ones; they take language itself as a prime subject and most often catalyze vision from a previous text explicitly invoked in the poem (or, with Browning, from a work of art in another medium explicitly described with literary terminology). And second, the Victorian poems display a greater textual defensiveness against their own vision, as though the speakers (and behind them, the poets) lacked even the Romantics' ambivalent confidence in their own imaginations. The later poets, that is, deploy their own textuality both to provoke and to proscribe their visions.

The climactic ninety-fifth section of Tennyson's elegy *In Memoriam* illustrates the Victorian variations. The poem accords with Greater Romantic Lyrics in its determinate speaker in a particular landscape (the grounds outside the house) who moves through a three-part structure of description, vision, and evaluation. The vision stems from an explicit, literary inspiration, in this case the speaker's reading of Hallam's letters, arrived at by association with the "fallen leaves" of the landscape. It culminates Tennyson's well-known tendency to perceive Hallam in linguistic terms, as in "the letters of thy name" on the tablet in section 67, "the sentence that he speaks" in 80, or "the flowery walk / Of letters" in 84. Whereas Tennyson refers to his dead friend in terms of both written and oral language, he tends to associate speech with memory and written texts with vision. That happens in section 95, too, where the first and third parts stress oral language: "While now we sang old songs that peal'd / From knoll to knoll" and "A breeze . . . said, / 'The dawn, the dawn.'" But the visionary middle part instead emphasizes textuality. Here it is:

> A hunger seized my heart; I read
>   Of that glad year which once had been,
>   In those fallen leaves which kept their green,
> The noble letters of the dead:

And strangely on the silence broke
    The silent-speaking words, and strange
    Was love's dumb cry defying change
To test his worth; and strangely spoke

The faith, the vigour, bold to dwell
    On doubts that drive the coward back,
    And keen through wordy snares to track
Suggestion to her inmost cell.

So word by word, and line by line,
    The dead man touched me from the past,
    And all at once it seemed at last
The living soul was flashed on mine,

And mine in this was wound, and whirled
    About empyreal heights of thought,
    And came on that which is, and caught
The deep pulsations of the world,

Aeonian music measuring out
    The steps of Time—The shocks of Chance—
    The blows of Death. At length my trance
Was cancelled, stricken through with doubt.[5]

That vision both derives from a source acknowledged as literary—the letters—and takes language itself as subject. By contemplating the letters, with their "silent-speaking words" strangely discoursing of love, faith, and doubt, Tennyson "word by word, and line by line" arrives at the famous vision of Hallam's soul momentarily flashed on his. He even announces the end of vision in terms of literary composition: At length the trance "Was cancelled, stricken through with doubt." Unlike the romantic stress on language in the third or evaluative section (as with Keats's "Forlorn! the very word . . ."), Tennyson displays an extraordinary linguistic self-consciousness during the vision itself and even derives that visionary experience from a literary source explicitly acknowledged in the poem. The Greater Romantic Lyric closest to Tennyson's procedure is Coleridge's "The Nightingale," with its citation of Milton's description of the nightingale in "Il Penseroso" as "most musical, most melancholy." But Coleridge's poem explicitly begins with a natural setting and only invokes Milton's text in order to rebut it and show instead the superiority of direct perception of nature over textual mediation as a path to "joy." That direct perception depends upon orality: *hearing* the nightingale's song against *reading* Milton's text, in the very work that Coleridge labelled "a conversation poem."

Again unlike his predecessors, Tennyson displays considerable defensiveness against the power of vision. To begin with, in contrast to the present-tense immediacy of their experience, he distances the entire episode by relating his poem entirely in the past tense. Second, the exact repetitions in the opening and closing sections suggest less a rounding of the poem on itself than a denial of the vision, before and after which the poem tells us that "couched at ease, / The white kine glimmered, and the trees / Laid their dark arms about the field." Whereas Keats in the Nightingale ode genuinely wonders whether he has experienced a vision or a dream, Tennyson more firmly declares his trance "cancelled, stricken through with doubt." And finally, such change as the poem allows comes not in the speaker directly, but only through his description of the landscape. After the repetition of the lines about the white kine, the poem does describe a landscape altered from night to day and from calm to wind. Characteristically, Tennyson suggests change only through projection onto a psychological landscape.

The experience clearly matches Tennyson's own prose account of recurrent visionary moments in his life, as recorded in his son's memoir: "A kind of waking trance I have frequently had, quite up from boyhood, when I have been all alone. This has generally come upon me thro' repeating my own name two or three times to myself silently, till all at once, as it were out of the intensity of the consciousness of individuality, the individuality itself seemed to dissolve and fade away into boundless being."[6] This account, too, begins with a linguistic stimulus to vision, and even the phrase "fade away into boundless being" finds its echo in "broaden into boundless day" from the poem. The phraseology here may owe something to the light imagery of Wordsworth's "Intimations Ode." Yet Tennyson, unlike Wordsworth, refuses to integrate the visionary experience with his more ordinary powers and was even more troubled than Wordsworth by the potential clash of his vision with Christian orthodoxy. Instead, he erects a series of defenses to keep it discrete, discontinuous, and distanced. As late as

1872 he continued to tinker with the diction to assuage his uneasy conscience.[7]

For all his differences with Tennyson, Matthew Arnold displayed the same linguistic self-consciousness and defenses against his own vision whenever he approached Greater Romantic Lyric. His most ambitious poem along those lines, "The Scholar-Gypsy," affords a nearly symmetric structure of three introductory verses locating the Arnoldian speaker in a landscape near Oxford, ten more visionary ones culminating in a glimpse of the Scholar-Gypsy himself, ten evaluative ones in which the speaker returns to his own world (a shift signalled by the Keatsian "But what—I dream!"), and a final two stanzas on the Tyrian trader. Arnold, like Wordsworth in "Tintern Abbey" or Coleridge in "Frost at Midnight," thus attaches a fourth or final "in" section to the tripartite out-in-out movement. Appropriately, he responds to the architectonics as well as individualities of his romantic models.

Arnold, too, derives his vision from an explicitly literary experience, in his case a reading of Joseph Glanvil's 1661 treatise *The Vanity of Dogmatizing,* which he invokes in the first stanza of the vision section:

> And near me on the grass lies Glanvil's book—
> Come, let me read the oft-read tale again!
> The story of the Oxford scholar poor,
> Of pregnant parts and quick inventive brain,
> Who, tired of knocking at preferment's door,
> One summer-morn forsook
> His friends, and went to learn the gipsy-lore,
> And roam'd the world with that wild brotherhood,
> And came, as most men deem'd, to little good,
> But came to Oxford and his friends no more.[8]

This incorporation of an explicit literary stimulus to vision into the poem matches the role of Hallam's letters in *In Memoriam* 95. Arnold carefully emphasizes the textual stimulus to vision three times in the first three lines—first as "Glanvil's book," then as "the oft-read tale," and finally as "the story." This exceeds even the invocation of Sophocles at the start of the vision section in "Dover Beach" or the famous simile of the darkling plain at the end (derived from a passage in Thucydides which Arnold had to memorize as a schoolboy at Rugby). His defensiveness against the vision also recalls Tennyson and here takes two major forms. First, the speaker again puts his climactic glimpse of the gypsy on the winter road entirely in the past tense ("Have I not pass'd . . . ?"), which as in Tennyson creates a sense of distance and which Arnold compounds by slipping into an interrogative. And second, the speaker's synopsis of the Gypsy passage in Glanvil's book omits mention of the power that figure sought to learn from his companions, which Glanvil explicitly calls "the power of imagination."9 Arnold would advocate that power no more than Tennyson, and when Tennyson himself finally enters "The Scholar-Gypsy" he only "takes dejectedly / His seat upon the intellectual throne; / And all his store of sad experience he / Lays bare of wretched days."

But Arnold's speaker has a surprise in store for us, the final two stanzas where he plunges back "in" to create the memorable image of the Tyrian trader:

> Then fly our greetings, fly our speech and smiles!
> —As some grave Tyrian trader, from the sea,
> Descried at sunrise an emerging prow
> Lifting the cool-hair'd creepers stealthily,
> The fringes of a southward-facing brow
> Among the Ægæan isles;
> And saw the merry Grecian coaster come,
> Freighted with amber grapes, and Chian wine,
> Green, bursting figs, and tunnies steep'd in brine—
> And knew the intruders on his ancient home,
>
> The young light-hearted masters of the waves—
> And snatch'd his rudder, and shook out more sail;
> And day and night held on indignantly
> O'er the blue Midland waters with the gale,
> Betwixt the Syrtes and soft Sicily,
> To where the Atlantic raves
> Outside the western straits; and unbent sails
> There, where down cloudy cliffs, through sheets of foam,
> Shy traffickers, the dark Iberians come;
> And on the beach undid his corded bales.

In his strength and indignation the Tyrian trader corrects the flaws of the more frail Scholar-Gypsy even as he too consorts with those outcasts from civilization, the dark Iberians. On the one hand, the ability to imagine such a figure suggests that the speaker does still have imaginative resources to deploy against fevered modern civilization. But on the other hand, the content of this vision embodies the strength only to shun rather than to confront the changing contemporary order. Arnold deploys the Tyrian trader as a counterweight to Greek and, implicitly, English civilization, but we may remember (as Arnold would have from his biblical studies) that the biblical King Solomon made extensive use of Tyrian traders not only to extend his own empire but also to furnish the wood for the Temple and to adorn it (1 Kings 5–7). So, too, did Robert Browning think of both Tyrian traders and King Solomon in a poem called "Popularity," where he pondered the vagaries of postromantic tradition, particularly in the line of Keats.

In "Popularity" Browning aimed at a portrait of a "true poet."[10] The portrait turned out to involve a complex meditation on tradition. Browning began the effort to "draw you as you stand" with four stanzas on "Tyre the old" and its famous dye derived from the murex (a shellfish): "Who has not heard how Tyrian shells / Enclosed the blue, that dye of dyes . . . ?" He then connected Tyrian trading in the dye to Solomon's architectural labor:

> Enough to furnish Solomon
> Such hangings for his cedar-house
> That, when gold-robed he took the throne
> In that abyss of blue, the Spouse
> Might swear his presence shone.

After that passage Browning jumps to the present in the kind of juxtaposition that Ezra Pound would later admire. The story of Tyre and Solomon becomes an ironic parable for the nineteenth century, in which Browning sees his Victorian contemporaries exploiting for wealth and fame the discoveries which Romantics like Keats worked out with scant reward. In contrast to the success of the generic "Hobbs, Nobbs, Stokes and Nokes," Browning asks, "Who fished the murex up? / What porridge had John Keats?"

Browning invoked Solomon by name again at the start of his own revision of Greater Romantic Lyric in "Abt Vogler," a poem that he regarded as central enough to his achievement to name in 1885 as one of two lyrics that would "represent their writer fairly."[11] "Abt Vogler" followed the familiar tripartite structure but substituted an art—in this case, music—for nature, in the manner of Keats before the Grecian Urn. Again, a Victorian reworking of a romantic form begins with explicit evocation within the poem of a previous literary text, in this case Talmudic commentary on the supreme text of the Bible. Like Tennyson and Arnold, Browning defends against the power of full vision by putting his poem in the past tense. Further, in the poem we do not see the musician Vogler soar "higher still and higher" (like Shelley's Skylark) but rather watch him modulate into memory of Roman fireworks. With his cult of imperfection and the transitory moment, Browning avoided what he saw as a fixed and therefore false permanence in some romantic vision. Here in the sixth stanza Vogler claims the superiority of music to both painting and verse, as media for recording vision, precisely on the grounds that music does not leave such a fixity: "for think, had I painted the whole / Why, there it had stood, to see, nor the process so wonder-worth: / Had I written the same, made verse . . ." Vogler rejoices *because* his "palace" is "gone," and in the last stanza he subsides, "Well, it is earth with me." But unlike Vogler, Browning has written a poem, which stands for us to see, and that poem tells us that there was a vision but declines to show it to us directly.

Because of his allegiance to the display of "Action in Character"[12] in the dramatic monologue, Browning did not approach the Greater Romantic Lyric as closely as did Tennyson and Arnold, but like "Abt Vogler" his other close approximations share the same double bent to begin by invoking texts and to shy off from espousal of full vision. In Browning, the previous texts are as often pictures as poems, but he takes care to describe the pictures in literary terminology, matching a general Victorian habit to the particular needs of reworking a literary genre. In one of his earliest and structurally simplest examples, "My Last Duchess," the Duke prominently begins by stressing the necessity to "read" the portrait (line 6). That poem displays a straightforward three-part structure of description-vision-evaluation accompanied by a displacement in time (now-then-now). The Duke begins with present description, modulates into a vision section based on memory, and returns to the present scene in his palace. But in the central section the Duke's prodigious memory performs a grotesque parody of a memory-powered Wordsworthian vision, just as Childe Roland will when he looks within only to discover memories of the traitors Cuthbert and

Giles. "The Englishman in Italy," which begins with the speaker describing a landscape before "telling my memories over," ends with reference to parliamentary debates over the Corn Law in England. "Old Pictures in Florence" again brings its own stimulus into the poem when the speaker urges us, "See Vasari." In these and other poems the speakers insist on rendering aesthetic perception in textual terms, whatever art they consider.

We can now see that "Pictor Ignotus," discussed in the previous chapter, shares both the linguistic stress and defensive strategies of Browning's other variations on Greater Romantic Lyric. Typically for Browning, its initiatory texts are paintings rather than poems or prose (it begins in reaction to the rival's pictures) rendered in linguistic terms and calling forth linguistic response. In this poem pictures "proclaim" (line 16) to us, and a variety of voices respond. Even the content of the central vision section culminates in a scene of linguistic instruction, in which age "greet[s]" the painter and youth lies learning at his feet; both surround him with "praise." The architectonics of the poem expand the three-part romantic structure to five: Initial statement and description yield to the vignettes of Hope, Rapture, and Confidence, which in turn generate the central vision not of the imagined painting itself but rather of response to it; after that, the pictor recoils from his vision through the associative derangement of the "voice" and "faces," which he compares to idolatrous revels and the rape of a nun, until he subsides again into ordinary rationalizations at the end. The governing of the syntax by negatives and his flight from his own vision conspire to make the discourse itself reenact the failure of his larger career. They thus place a defensive frame around the vision even in the act of presenting it. For all his variations, Browning's approaches to Greater Victorian Lyric share both the psychological ambivalence and linguistic defenses of both Tennyson and Arnold.

The Greater Victorian Lyric needs to be distinguished not only from similar romantic poems on the one hand but also from analogous modern ones on the other. T. S. Eliot and W. B. Yeats can serve as the two best exemplars. Each refashioned the Greater Romantic Lyric form to serve his own contemporary needs, Eliot in "Gerontion" and "East Coker I" and Yeats in several of his greatest works between 1918 and 1929, including "The Second Coming" and the second part of "The Tower." Surprisingly, of the two, Eliot comes closer to repeating the variations of the Greater Victorian Lyric, from which he departs chiefly in style. Yeats, in contrast, preserves the high style of both the Romantics and the Victorians even while refashioning the structure and content of his poetic inheritance.

Eliot's "Gerontion" presents a Greater Victorian Lyric in modernist stylistic guise. For all the variations of Eliot's compressed, allusive style and leaps in juxtaposition (both of which out-Browning Browning), he preserves the Victorian stresses on the textual stimulus to vision and on the defense against its powers through explicitly linguistic means. "Gerontion" really begins with two texts. The title suggests Newman's "Dream of Gerontius" even as the epigraph brings these lines from Shakespeare's *Measure for Measure* into the poem: "Thou hast nor youth nor age / But as it were an after dinner sleep / Dreaming of both." It was Shakespeare, of course, whom Arnold cautioned against imitating, lest poets follow his individual excellences but neglect *architectonicè*. Eliot solves that problem by dressing a nineteenth-century form in modern guise. The textual stimulus of his discourse continues in its opening lines: "Here I am, an old man in a dry month, / Being read to by a boy . . ."[13] Those lines not only emphasize the act of reading but also derive with slight change from a book that Eliot actually read, A. C. Benson's biography *Edward FitzGerald*. The poem could hardly evoke its textual origins more clearly. As it proceeds, the introductory array of Newman, Shakespeare, and Benson yields in turn to Lancelot Andrewes's *Nativity Sermon*, the Bible, *The Education of Henry Adams*, Thomas Middleton's *The Changeling*, Ben Jonson's *The Alchemist*, and George Chapman's *Bussy D'Ambois*. Some of those references function more as allusion than as incitement to vision, but the point is that the poem never lets us forget its own textuality.

Like its associational structure, the poem's textuality forms part of its defense against the power of imaginative vision, which always both fascinated and frightened Eliot. As Gerontion progresses from his opening, descriptive discourse through his associations to the Bible, the false devotions of Mr. Silvero and the others, the courtesan-like deceitfulness of history, and the vision of De Bailhache, Fresca, and Mrs. Cammel whirled beyond the Bear—with its paired lyricism of the gull against the wind—the dense intertextuality continually snares his associative and imaginative leaps into a framework of order, the key value Eliot always proclaimed in literary tradition. Similarly, the very reliance on association distances Gerontion from his own imaginative experience, so that he subsides at the end into the same "dry brain in a dry season" that he displayed at the beginning. None of the Victorians integrated psychological change based on imaginative vision into their speakers in the genre I have been considering: Tennyson displaced change onto a psychological landscape, Arnold only implied it through the Tyrian trader image, and neither Abt Vogler nor Pictor Ignotus is different at the end of his poem from what he was at the beginning. Eliot uses juxtaposition for the same end. More meditatively, he would repeat his Victorian variations in the first section of "East Coker." Eliot's stylistic innovations mask a deep affinity, and it is not surprising that he wrote an admiring essay on *In Memoriam*.

Tennyson's masterpiece always evoked the antipathy of the greatest modern reviser of Greater Romantic Lyric, W. B. Yeats, who adapted that form for major mature poems like "In Memory of Major Robert Gregory," "All Souls' Night," "The Second Coming," "The Double Vision of Michael Robartes," "The Tower, II," and "Coole Park, 1929." While continuing the nineteenth-century movement from colloquial to more elevated diction within such poems, Yeats refused either to ground his vision in textuality or to shy away from its imaginative content. Instead, his characteristic innovations include increasing the importance of vision over nature (thus divorcing his work from the Romantics) and redefining vision as the explicit summoning of images to the mind's eye (thus separating it from the textualizing Victorians as well). Sometimes he summons those images from the dead (Robert Gregory), sometimes from Spiritus Mundi (the rough beast), and sometimes from the surrounding landscape (Coole Park). Always he welcomes their appearance as a guarantee of his own imaginative power.

As I consider Yeats's revisions of Greater Romantic Lyric in the next chapter, I should like to close here not with one of them, but rather with "Solomon and the Witch," one of the moving poems he wrote for his wife shortly after their marriage. Tennyson had alluded briefly to the meeting of Solomon and Sheba in discussing relations between the sexes in *The Princess* (II, lines 325f.), but Yeats creates a more extensive dialogue between those representatives of male and female wisdom. In the poem he presents a Greater Romantic Lyric that wasn't, modulating the form into a comic account of a visionary apocalypse that doesn't quite come off. Sheba frames the poem with her description of the moon and grass that comprise the landscape setting. In between, Solomon thinks that "He that crowed out eternity / Thought to have crowed it in again" and that he and Sheba have through their lovemaking found a "real image" capable of reconciling sublunary opposites.[14] To Solomon's energetic rant of victorious vision, Sheba replies simply, "Yet the world stays." The staying of the world did not invalidate the imaginative enterprise for Yeats, any more than it did for the poets before him. "Solomon and the Witch" plays at apocalypse through imaginative images with a breezy confidence possible only to a poet secure both in his vision and in his relation to tradition. And despite the ultimate derivation of his characters from the account in 1 Kings 10, Yeats carefully proscribes textual stimulus from his poem. He saw that he could not simply repeat either his romantic or his Victorian forerunners but needed to develop from them in a distinctive art and architectonics of his own. He, as much as Tennyson, Browning, or Arnold, could characterize his own enterprise with Sheba's closing line: "O! Solomon! let us try again."

5 Yeats and the
Greater Romantic Lyric

In the second part of "The Tower" Yeats—as persona—paces on the battlements of his tower, stares at the landscape, and sends imagination forth to encounter it. That series of actions dramatically places him in a central romantic line of symbol, theme, and form; like Thoor Ballylee itself the poem becomes an elaborate stage set for Yeats to sport upon in his true role of modern Romantic. The tower as symbol derives partly from Shelley, as Yeats acknowledged in the related "Blood and the Moon": "And Shelley had his towers, thought's crowned powers he called them once."[1] Yeats adopted both the symbol itself and the notion of varying it from poem to poem which he found in his precursor. Correspondingly, "The Tower" seizes upon the high romantic theme of mind encountering the world through imagination. And finally, the second part of "The Tower"—and indeed the whole poem, for the underlying pattern would hold even without the overt triple division—is a Greater Romantic Lyric, in which poetic movement follows a special course of imaginative mental action. Yeats discovered his great mature subject in his relation to what "The Tower" calls "images and memories," and a characteristic means of developing it in the Greater Romantic Lyric. This essay first maps four romantic poems particularly pertinent to Yeats's endeavor, then pursues Yeats's reworking of Greater Romantic Lyric in "The Tower, II" and finally surveys his other innovations in that form. In focusing primarily on later poems I do not mean to scant Yeats's early romanticism but simply assume that topic to be sufficiently established already.[2] My subject here is Yeats's transformation of a romantic mode—and accompanying romantic themes—in some of his finest mature work, including "The Tower," "In Memory of Major Robert Gregory," and "The Second Coming."

Four representative Greater Romantic Lyrics serve as reference points for charting the grounds on which Yeats built his tower vision— Coleridge's "Frost at Midnight," Wordsworth's "Tintern Abbey," and Keats's "Ode to a Nightingale" and "Ode on a Grecian Urn." Situation, use of memory, and two structural innovations point our attention in "Frost at Midnight," which is in effect a Prayer for My Son. Like Yeats's "A Prayer for My Daughter," a variant on the pattern whose combination of the Atlantic with "Gregory's wood and one bare hill" recalls Coleridge's "sea, hill, and wood," the poem invokes growth in a future environment favorable to imagination for the poet's child, in contrast to the father's own experience. Coleridge's poem opens with a favorite Yeatsian situation—a man meditating at midnight inside his rural home, as in "All Souls' Night" or the more generally nocturnal "In Memory of Major Robert Gregory," two more of Yeats's Greater Romantic Lyrics. Unlike "Eolian Harp," this poem shifts into memory for its first "in" section, where Coleridge creates an image of his past self in remembering dreams prompted by a grate in childhood. Structurally, the vision comes in two parts punctuated by a return to the present, here a brief address to his "Dear Babe," before imagining a future of Hartley's communion with "lovely shapes and sounds intelligible." As Yeats will later sometimes do, Coleridge ends within his vision in impressive rhetoric.

"Tintern Abbey" follows "Frost at Midnight" in offering two visions, making the pattern out-in-out and then back in again, and stresses memory as much as imagination. As in "Coole Park, 1929" (a structurally simpler Greater Romantic Lyric) and in "The Wild Swans at Coole" (which in its original stanzaic order tried to be one as far as its theme of failed imagination would permit), dynamism derives from confrontation with a place important to the speaker in the past. Wordsworth first describes the scene, then imagines a near past when he remembered it and a further past when he first encountered it, comes back to the present, and then imagines a future for Dorothy. His diction rather than his technique of using memory to prepare for imaginative action claims our attention here. He speaks of animated mental images—"the picture of the mind," "beauteous forms," and being "laid asleep in body and become a living soul"—just as Coleridge calls on "flitting phantasies" and "shapings of the unregenerate mind." Although Yeats would have hated the poem's praise of nature, he habitually used similar phrases,[3] most notably "the mind's eye," and interpreted romantic references to images, phantoms, and other shapes more literally than their creators did. The point is not that he borrowed terms from, say, Wordsworth, but that a drive to render similar mental action causes related phraseology among writers in this genre.

Keats's two odes return to a normative three-part pattern with obvious links to Yeats's later work but also with those differences of stance which made Yeats cleave more unto Shelley. Unlike Yeats, Keats remains in the present tense, for his poems depict an ongoing struggle to transform current experience rather than to invoke memory. "Ode to a Nightingale" speaks a parable of sympathetic imagination—first bodily quiescence, then imaginative projection into the nightingale ("already with thee"), and final collapse of the vision with a bell-like forlorn "to toll me back from thee to my sole self." This Keatsian out-in-out pattern of interaction with a natural object remained alien to Yeats, who created visions apart from nature. In the Byzantium poems, his desire to reincarnate himself in a golden bird of art both recalls and "corrects" Keats's limitation of merger within natural rather than aesthetic boundaries. But even while divorcing human life from cold pastoral, Keats did allow his imagination to interact with art. In "Ode on a Grecian Urn" he first describes the urn (out), then enters into his vision to imagine a town not actually on the urn (in) at his highest intensity, and then withdraws again to a more distanced perspective (out). That is, he substitutes an artwork for an actual landscape to prompt his Greater Romantic Lyric, as Wordsworth did in "Elegiac Stanzas" on Peele Castle. Yeats does not, though poems like " A Bronze Head" or "The Municipal Gallery Revisited" display similar devices. Most strikingly, his imagining of the Chinamen arriving at the halfway house in "Lapis Lazuli" parallels Keats's image of the Grecian town—neither scene exists in the artistic object, but only in the poet's mind. Yeats took from Keats as much as he could without changing from creative to sympathetic imagination.

The Romantics channeled so much creative energy into the new genre because it followed the shape of imaginative experience. More than displaying the results of imaginative creation, it allowed the following through of a mind moving from description or ordinary perception to vision and then back again. Abrams has quoted Coleridge on the return upon itself as a device making for wholeness: "The common end of all *narrative*, nay, of *all*, Poems . . . is to convert a *series* into a *Whole:* to make those events, which in real or imagined History move on in a *strait* Line, assume to our Understandings a *circular* motion—the snake with it's Tail in its Mouth."[4] Experience thus assumes the shape of ouroboros, the tail-eating snake. Equally important, it becomes a cycle and harmonizes with the cyclicity that haunts romantic thought (as it does Yeats's own) about both societies and individuals. Often this cyclicity takes a special shape: Vision breaks off at its intensest moment and the poet returns to his ordinary state, whether in "The Eolian Harp," "Grecian Urn," or "Nightingale." Inability to sustain imagination in the poems matches our experience in life. Wordsworth minimized the discrepancy and drew new strength from his experience, while Keats stressed the discontinuity. At his most extreme a Keatsian poet is not sure which state is real, the imaginative or the ordinary, and is plagued by doubt and questioning, often ending the poem with an interrogative ("Do I wake or sleep?"). Yet despite the persona's questions, these poems ratify vision de facto, for in all of them vision is more important than natural landscape. The poems exist to present the visions, and interest centers on acts of mind, not narrative description of nature. Significance springs only from mind—the landscapes do not possess meaning in themselves but only that meaning which the poet gives them by his own mental processes. The banks of the Wye interest us only because of Wordsworth's experiences there, and we do not know at all from the poem precisely where Keats encounters his nightingale.

Yeats wrote Greater Romantic Lyrics only in his maturity, when he had cast off derivative romanticism of the nineties and was creating a modern variety. The form suited the intermittent pulsations of his own imagination, and its circular shape harmonized with his antinomies and gyres. By moving into and then out of vision he could hold in a single poem reality and justice, or actual and ideal. Likewise, doubts generated by discontinuity between states matched his own vacillations. Yet he did not simply imitate his romantic predecessors. Instead, he stepped up the importance of vision over nature even further, diminishing description of external scene and preserving only as much of nature as imagination needed. For him vision became a literal summoning of images in nature's spite. In effect, he crossed visionary autonomy from Blake and Shelley with poetic structure from Words-worth, Coleridge, and Keats. That maneuver freed him from the Victorians as well: He could embrace determinedly the visionary power that they sought to evade defensively, and he would derive his vision more from visual images than from textual inscriptions. The resultant hybrids included many of his best poems between 1918 and 1929.

"The Tower" (VP 409) makes the form an arena for a romantic grappling with the despondency of aging. Unlike Wordsworth, the poet still has both flaming imagination and fervent sense. For Blake, those would have been enough,[5] but Yeats here fears waning of emo-tion, the third term he introduced into his exposition of Blake. His temptation is abstract argument, for his years demand the philosophic mind, which he conquers through vision. The first five lines of part two present an orthodox beginning for a Greater Romantic Lyric: A speaker looks at a landscape and "send[s] imagination forth" to encounter it. The next line signals a Yeatsian innovation, in calling "images and memories" from the landscape. Were the speaker Keats, he would identify with objects in the scene; were he Wordsworth, he would summon images and memories of his past self. Since he is Yeats, he calls up images and memories mostly of others. With their arrival the "in" part of the lyric begins.

These images divide the great symbols of passion and mood Yeats admired in the Romantics into paired creator and follower—Mrs. French and her serving man, blind poet Raftery and the man drowned in Cloone bog, and Yeats's own characters of old juggler and tricked Hanrahan. Despite his Shelleyan situation on the tower, Yeats here repudiates his youthful Intellectual vision of ascent to the ideal which he had founded upon Shelley. Mrs. French's servant, the drowned man, and Hanrahan all carry over ideal moonlit visions into the actual world ("the prosaic light of day") and so end in disaster. Opposed to that, Yeats now wants moon and sunlight to "seem / One inextricable beam" encompassing antinomies into which all things fall without kindling a mad lust to live only by the moon.

The vision builds to its climax in Yeats's questioning of those images of passion—did they too rage against old age as he does? Just here, in line 101, we suddenly realize what Yeats has done. He has called up the images literally, and they stand in front of him:

But I have found an answer in those eyes
That are impatient to be gone;
Go, therefore; but leave Hanrahan.

We understand that Wordsworth imagines his past self near Tintern
Abbey, or that Keats imagines himself with the nightingale; but what
are we to understand by Yeats addressing images here as though they
were present? We can make sense of this in two ways: First, he has
slipped into reverie, and these images "in the Great Memory stored"
(line 85) have now entered his individual consciousness. If we do not
believe in the Great Memory, then we can say that he has called up
images from his own conscious or subconscious memory (Yeats in fact
knew a fair amount about the characters in this poem), or else simply
created them outright, and in the intensity of his vision addresses them
as if they were present, which they are in the mind.

Whatever explanation we choose, the speaker modulates out of
vision in questioning Hanrahan, his own creation. His second question
signals the change: "Does the imagination dwell the most / Upon a
woman won or woman lost?" The "you" in the following line refers
more to Yeats himself than to Hanrahan, for this is another of Yeats's
continual self-reproaches about his failed relation to Maud Gonne.
The lines of the poem,

If on the lost, admit you turned aside
From a great labyrinth out of pride,
Cowardice, some silly over-subtle thought
Or anything called conscience once . . .

parallel the mixture of pride, timidity, over-subtlety, and conscience in
a passage about Maud in the original draft of his autobiography:

And in all that followed I was careful to touch [her] as one
might a sister. If she was to come to me, it must be from no
temporary passionate impulse, but with the approval of her
conscience. Many a time since then, as I lay awake at night,
have I accused myself of acting, not as I thought from a high
scruple, but from a dread of moral responsibility, and my

thoughts have gone round and round, as do miserable
thoughts, coming to no solution.[6]

That love, linked by Yeats to his early romanticism, signifies the same
mistake made by the servant, drowned man, and even Hanrahan, yet
its memory is so strong that even the memory reduces him to their
condition. With realization in the poem that passion still remembers
what was so fugitive, Yeats's obstinate questionings cease. Yet in mak-
ing this tangent to the "Intimations Ode" he veers off into his own
orbit, for he refuses the Wordsworthian comfort of the philosophic
mind and, spurred by the renewed sense of loss on which his poetry
depends, makes his will in triumph of imagination. Exaltation carries
over into the third section, until it subsides again in the closing lines
and leaves the poet where he began, though with a difference.

The images summoned in this poem provide one gauge for Yeats's
claim to have corrected romanticism by fastening its visions to a
national landscape, and thus reinvigorating them. Unlike Greater
Romantic Lyrics of the Romantics themselves, "The Tower" could not
be transferred to another setting. Mrs. French, Raftery, and Mary
Hines, the bankrupt ancient master of the house, and others all lived in
this landscape. Yeats's elevation of major and minor Irish figures into
heroic roles has stirred a large controversy in which both its defenders
and its attackers overstate their cases. On the one hand, Yeats's allu-
sions to Mary Hines, or, say, to Maeve, do not make his poems any
easier for non-Irish readers (and perhaps not always even for Irish
ones); they are, in fact, obstacles to understanding. On the other hand,
critics who simply condemn the habit, and Yeats's exaggerated claims
for it, miss the point. In "The Tower" he uses them to move away from
romantic subjectivity, which made earlier Greater Romantic Lyrics
depend only upon the poets' minds and not their environments. Mrs.
French and Raftery, or elsewhere MacGregor Mathers or William
Horton, are not immediately meaningful for everybody, but they do, at
least, link private vision to something beyond the poet himself. In *A
Vision* Yeats boasted that he had improved on Blake by turning histor-
ical characters into elements of his mythology and so made it more
accessible. A romanticist might respond with some truth that the
representativeness of Wordsworth's or Keats's mind makes them in fact
more accessible than Yeats's quirky Celts, but I think it also true that

Yeats's poems do gain both force and a measure of seeming imperson-
ality from his tactic, which the character of his imagination badly
needed. Though original Romantics may not have required this attach-
ment, Yeats himself clearly did.

Yeats habitually addresses such images as if they were present and
often claims that he sees them "in the mind's eye." That phrase takes us
back to Hamlet, not thin from eating flies but as visionary prince:

> Hamlet: My father—methinks I see my father.
> Horatio: O, where, my lord?
> Hamlet: In my mind's eye, Horatio.

Yeats used the expression particularly often from about the time of
Responsibilities through *The Tower*, when it appears in half a dozen
poems and frequently in his prose. He connected it especially to seeing
images of human forms, for which the allusion to Hamlet provides a
cunning context. In Shakespeare's play Hamlet uses his mind's eye to
see a mental image of his dead father, but he is shortly to encounter a
real ghost. In Yeats's poems speakers summon figures which could be
mental images but which also seem, like ghosts, to exist independently.
The Shakespearian echo allows us to interpret the images as we choose,
with Yeats himself remaining as gnomic as the Delphic oracle.

Because Yeats's chief innovation in the Greater Romantic Lyric was
to make vision into a summoning of images, we need to look more
closely at these images seen in the mind's eye before turning to more of
his work in that genre. They are usually great figures of passion or of
mood, like the romantic questers so dear to Yeats. We meet the first as a
completed poet-figure associated with a tower in a sort of Greater
Romantic Lyric in prose, related as an incident from a tour of the
Apennines:

> I was alone amid a visionary, fantastic, impossible scenery.
> It was sunset and the stormy clouds hung upon mountain
> after mountain, and far off on one great summit a cloud
> darker than the rest glimmered with lightning. Away south
> upon another mountain a mediaeval tower, with no build-
> ing near nor any sign of life, rose into the clouds. I saw
> suddenly in the mind's eye an old man, erect and a little
> gaunt, standing in the door of the tower, while about him

broke a windy light. He was the poet who had at last, because he had done so much for the world's sake, come to share in the dignity of the saint.[7]

Yeats goes on to combine the figure with Jesus in an ecstatic rhapsody in which the old man, a mixture of Athanase and Ahasuerus, becomes a prototype of the poet as successful quester and mage. The passage's embryonic doctrine of poet and mask exfoliates later in "Ego Dominus Tuus" (1917), where Hic argues that Dante "made that hollow face of his / More plain to the mind's eye than any face / But that of Christ" (VP 368). Ille's correction of Hic's oversimple account of how poets create their masks concerns us less than how the masks or images are perceived by observers—in the mind's eye as figures of impassioned questing.

Three other poems in which images appear to the mind's eye ring changes on the theme of intense desire. In "The Magi" (1914) they are searching again for the divine union of celestial mystery and bestial floor, while in the last section of "Meditations in Time of Civil War" (1923) they are troopers calling for vengeance on the murderers of Jacques Molay. Clearly, the images can represent misdirected as well as admired passion, for Yeats's note to "Meditations" identifies the troopers' cry as "fit symbol for those who labour for hatred, and so for sterility in various kinds" (VP 827). A mixed tone pervades the description of William Horton, first image summoned in the Greater Romantic Lyric "All Souls' Night" (1921). Like early Yeats, Horton had known "that sweet extremity of pride / That's called platonic love" (VP 471). After the death of his lady (Audrey Locke) he fixes "his mind's eye . . . on one sole image," a fusion of her and God.[8] Despite Yeats's ambivalence toward Horton's (and his own) form of quest, concentrated intensity still makes Horton fit auditor of the poem's "mummy truths."

Besides great figures of passion and mood, the mind's eye could summon figures of self-possessed mastery or symbols from esoteric Yeatsism. To the first group belong Major Robert Gregory and his literary forerunner, the fisherman. In "The Fisherman" Yeats calls up an image of a Connemara man who does not exist but is "a dream" as ideal audience for the cold and passionate poetry he wanted to write. Here Yeats gives us a simple account of his genesis—he simply imagined the man. His accounts of the origin of images were not always so direct, whether in poetry or in prose. The Great Memory which he invoked in "The Tower" and the Spiritus Mundi of "The Second Coming" found fuller description in *Per Amica Silentia Lunae*, where Yeats described his own practice of symbolic meditation:

> Before the mind's eye, whether in sleep or waking, came images that one was to discover presently in some book one had never read, and after looking in vain for explanation to the current theory of forgotten personal memory, I came to believe in a Great Memory passing on from generation to generation. But that was not enough, for these images showed intention and choice. . . . The thought was again and again before me that this study had created a contact or mingling with minds who had followed a like study in some other age. . . . Our daily thought was certainly but the line of foam at the shallow edge of a vast luminous sea; Henry More's *Anima Mundi*, Wordsworth's "immortal sea which brought us hither."[9]

The Great Memory gets into the poetry, but the guardedly expressed (not "I believed" but "the thought was before me") remainder does not, except possibly for the Spiritus Mundi of "The Second Coming." The sphinx vision there, like the related one seen by the mind's eye in "The Double Vision of Michael Robartes," will appear in our chronological survey of Yeats's Greater Romantic Lyrics. We have learned enough of the mind's eye and its images to continue.

Yeats wrote eight Greater Romantic Lyrics between 1918 and 1929. They divide into four pairs: "In Memory of Major Robert Gregory" (1918) and "All Souls' Night" (1921) summon images of the dead; "The Second Coming" (1920) and "The Double Vision of Michael Robartes" (1919) conjure images from the Great Memory; "The Tower, II" (1927) and "Meditations in Time of Civil War, VII" (1922) stress the tower top; and "Coole Park, 1929" (1931; written 1929) and "The Crazed Moon" (1932; written 1923) offer landscapes uncommonly symbolic even by Yeats's standards. All relate to romanticism in form and often in theme and symbol as well, as we saw in "The Tower." The earliest of them, "In Memory of Major Robert Gregory," prefigures both the tower symbol and the stanzaic pattern of that poem, for it takes place in the "ancient tower" and uses the same $a\,a\,b\,b\,c\,d\,d\,c$ rhyme scheme which Yeats derived from Cowley's elegiac ode on William Harvey and based two other romantic poems upon, "A Prayer for My Daughter" and "Byzantium." The Coleridgean situation of Yeats's elegy recalls "Frost at Midnight," while its place in the overall order of Yeats's poems recalls Shelley, for it follows "The Wild Swans at Coole," whose basic image derives from an encounter between poet and swan in *Alastor*.

Mental action in "In Memory of Major Robert Gregory" (VP 323) follows the program of description-vision-evaluation, but a brief return to the present divides the vision itself into two parts, one of Lionel Johnson, John Synge, and George Pollexfen, and the other of Robert Gregory himself. Typically, for Yeats, the vision reverts to the past, counterpointing the spatial out-in-out with a temporal present-past-present sequence. He begins with meditative description of his present situation in the tower, whose subdued symbolic suggestion still alerts us for imminent imagination. In the initial vision, images of "discoverers of forgotten truth" and "companions" come to the speaker's mind. All of them are figures of passion or mood: Johnson brooding on sanctity and dreaming of consummation, Synge finding at last an objective correlative to his heart in passionate and simple Aran islanders, and Pollexfen forsaking physical sport for astrological search. A relapse into the present to mention "all things the delighted eye now sees" prepares for the sustained vision of Robert Gregory. Though described as ideal "soldier, scholar, horseman," Gregory appears mostly as artist, particularly if we remember that the eighth stanza, on horsemanship, was added to the poem later at his widow's request. In accomplishing all "perfectly," Gregory resolves the split between active and contemplative, becoming the kind of possible subject for a poem suggested at the end of Stevens's "Of Modern Poetry." The vision culminates in the eleventh stanza, where Yeats subordinates Gregory to symbolic ignition of the combustible world. The question "What made us dream that he could comb grey hair?" signals the exhaustion of imagination at its intensest moment and prepares us to shift back "out" into evaluation.

The final stanza deserves more attention than it usually receives. Its first two lines, which return us to the original scene, oppose the wind of nature (not inspiration) to mind and suggest that mind creates its images to counterbalance nature, to resist a violence from without by a violence from within. The speaker then reveals his original plan—not just to call up Synge (whom "manhood tried"), Pollexfen (whom "childhood loved"), or Johnson (whom "boyish intellect approved"), but to *comment* on them "Until imagination brought / A fitter welcome." Imagination thus redeems the decay implicit in the chronological sequence love-approve-test. Yeats's always erratic punctuation obscures the syntax here. A comma instead of semicolon after "each" in the first two printings[10] makes it culminate the previous sequence—he thought to comment until imagination would enter in. This Yeats has done most fully for Gregory but also in miniature for Johnson, Synge, and Pollexfen, whom he has turned into images of intensity. But, the last two lines suggest, thought of Gregory's death interrupted a lengthier sequence by discharging Yeats's passion ("heart"). This exhaustion of the heart recurs as problem in "The Tower"; here it marks the end of a remarkable reworking of a romantic mode.

Similar structure holds together the more abstruse "All Souls' Night," written two years later and eventually made into an epilogue for *A Vision*. Again the speaker summons a trio of dead contemporaries—Horton, Florence (Farr) Emery, and MacGregor Mathers, all of whom appear as images of the esoteric students Yeats imitated as Athanase. Since the mental action resembles that of the Gregory elegy,[11] we may focus on the meaning of "the dead." In the earlier poem, the figures were dead in a double sense: They had physically died, and they had become artistic images in the poem, part of the artifice of eternity opposed to time. This Shelleyan association of death with completion or fulfillment, which had informed Yeats's poems of the nineties, spills over into "All Souls' Night," where the ghostly (a deliberate Yeatsian pun) images become fit auditors for Yeats's "mummy truths," both of the poem and of *A Vision*. As creations of imagination, they can share Yeats's own imaginative communications. As conclusion to the *Tower* volume, the poem neatly reverses the situation of the initial "Sailing to Byzantium," when Yeats had wanted to be instructed by the spirits; as a result of lessons learned in poems like "The Tower," he can now summon spirits to be instructed by him in imagination's truth. That is, the volume as a whole resurrects flagging passion and harnesses it to imaginative vision. A different kind of action informs the next pair of Yeats's Greater Romantic Lyrics.

Like "The Double Vision of Michael Robartes," Yeats's famous "The Second Coming" calls up impersonal images rather than those fashioned from the poet's past. Yeats ascribes their source to Spiritus Mundi, which in a note to another poem from *Michael Robartes and the Dancer* he defines as "a general storehouse of images which have ceased to be a property of any personality or spirit" (VP 822). The poem's brevity clearly reveals its structure as a Greater Romantic Lyric:

> Turning and turning in the widening gyre
> The falcon cannot hear the falconer;
> Things fall apart; the centre cannot hold;
> Mere anarchy is loosed upon the world,
> The blood-dimmed tide is loosed, and everywhere   5
> The ceremony of innocence is drowned;
> The best lack all conviction, while the worst
> Are full of passionate intensity.
> Surely some revelation is at hand;
> Surely the Second Coming is at hand.   10
> The Second Coming! Hardly are those words out
> When a vast image out of *Spiritus Mundi*
> Troubles my sight: somewhere in sands of the desert
> A shape with lion body and the head of a man,
> A gaze blank and pitiless as the sun,   15
> Is moving its slow thighs, while all about it
> Reel shadows of the indignant desert birds.
> The darkness drops again; but now I know
> That twenty centuries of stony sleep
> Were vexed to nightmare by a rocking cradle,   20
> And what rough beast, its hour come round at last,
> Slouches towards Bethlehem to be born?   (VP 401–2)

The transition from description to vision comes midway in line 11, while that from vision to evaluation occurs immediately after line 17. But here Yeats prepares for vision not by passive reverie or negative capability but by working himself into a prophetic frenzy. He adopts the stance of seer, and what he describes is not an actual landscape but a metaphoric one: We do not feel that a falcon flies off before his eyes any more than that he literally sees a blood-dimmed tide. Instead, he depicts the state of Europe as if from the top of a mile-high tower, from which he can see as far as the Germans in Russia—whom he mentioned in the original draft.[12] Scholarly quarrels about identity of falcon and falconer—whether Christ and man, nature and spirit, logic and mind—should not be allowed to obscure the emblem's significance, loss of control. It matches loss of rational control in the speaker's mental action as he moves to a rhetorical crescendo preparatory to vision.

Because the image seen in the mind's eye comes from Spiritus Mundi, Yeats does not have to recall it personally; consequently, he can increase urgency by writing the entire poem in the present tense. The vision section carries over the passionate tone of the quasi description to a displacement only in space and not in time. A here-there-here movement matches the familiar out-in-out structure. This vision of antithetical Egyptian Sphinx heralding the end of primary Christianity replaces the erratic falcon with birds once again wheeling in formation. Although Yeats often exults at the end of "scientific, democratic, fact-accumulating, heterogeneous civilization,"[13] commentators err in seeing that attitude in the poem. The vision "troubles" the speaker's sight; it is the sphinx whose eye is "blank and pitiless."

With the end of vision the speaker's return to himself completes the doubling action built into the poem by the paired birds, the title itself, and the repeated phrases "turning," "is loosed," "surely," "the Second Coming," and "is at hand." The change reminds us why the Greater Romantic Lyric attracted Yeats so much: Its return upon itself suits his true subject, which is more his relation to his vision than the vision itself. Typically, the vision leaves the speaker in a state of partial illumination. Now he knows not only that a nightmarish coming is at hand, but also that it was caused by the rocking cradle of Jesus. This means, I think, not just that the gyres are reciprocal (living each other's life and dying each other's death), but that the new god appears savage because seen through the mental set of Christian civilization and its derivatives. The final question is genuine, not rhetorical; in Yeats's system we know that something is coming, but we do not know precisely what, nor can we, for we are bound by the old civilization. Nor does the speaker rejoice, for his phrase "rough beast" suggests horror rather than delight.

"The Second Coming" is romantic in more than form; it is shot through with Blakean and Shelleyan echoes in theme and diction. Behind the poem lurks "Ozymandias," with its picture of a monumental ruin in a desert, while Harold Bloom has identified the source of the center which cannot hold in the rejection of natural love by the Witch of Atlas.[14] Likewise, the phrase "stony sleep" comes from Blake's *Book of Urizen,* where it describes Urizen's transitional phase between his Eternal state and his rebirth as fallen man.[15] But reworking of the Last Fury's speech in act one of *Prometheus Unbound* dwarfs even those in significance:

> The good want power, but to weep barren tears.
> The powerful goodness want: worse need for them.
> The wise want love; and those who love want wisdom;
> And all best things are thus confused to ill.   (ll. 625–28)

> The best lack all conviction, while the worst
> Are full of passionate intensity.   (VP 402)

As many commentators, including the present one,[16] have pointed out, Yeats reverses the thrust of Shelley's apocalyptic lines by making them a prelude to another cycle rather than to (possibly temporary) transfiguration. Here, we may note the difference in mental action. Prometheus frustrates the Fury's plan to torture him with a vision of human suffering by unexpectedly drawing strength from it: "The sights with which thou torturest gird my soul / With new endurance, till the hour arrives / When they shall be no types of things which are." A vision of heroic and selfless virtues follows in the songs of the six spirits, preparatory to the poem's later apocalypse of love. In "The Second Coming," however, the comparable lines create a frenzy in the speaker which prepares him for a vision of the rough beast to come, after which he reverts to his original state, having grown in knowledge but not in power. There is a fatalism in the poem which Yeats's *Vision* system often prompted, in which the quest for Unity of Being turns into a quest for knowledge instead, whether "mummy truths" of "All Souls' Night" or half-knowledge of "The Second Coming." Against this, Yeats sets ironic self-criticism as in "The Phases of the Moon" or images of Unity of Being like the dancer in "Among School Children."

"The Double Vision of Michael Robartes" (VP 382) summons images from Spiritus Mundi or the Great Memory and returns us to Yeats's concern with the poet's relation to Unity of Being. In a Greater Romantic Lyric which begins and ends in the ruins of a chapel restored on the Rock of Cashel by Cormac MacCarthy in the twelfth century, Robartes sees "in the mind's eye" two visions—in terms of the system, the first of phase one and the second of phase fifteen. In the second, a girl emblematic of Unity of Being dances between Sphinx (this time a Grecian one, representing knowledge) and Buddha (love). Because all three have overthrown time, like other images in Yeats they seem both dead and alive. In the third movement of the lyric (out), Robartes's attention focuses on the girl who "outdanced" thought. He identifies her with a dream maiden forgotten when awake, one of the Shelleyan ideals of Yeats's youth, whom in later life he preferred to identify with Homer's Helen or Dante's Beatrice. Unlike her, he is caught not between perfect knowledge and perfect love but rather in the human tension between objective thought and subjective images. He faces this predicament both in life and in the two opposing states which form the poem. With vision fled, his gain is knowledge of a personal ideal, not of impersonal forces as in "The Second Coming." Development toward that ideal is the one freedom offered by Yeats's system, though he allows others outside of it. The lyric ends with his romantic "moan" of recognition and equally romantic resolve to render the experience artistically. Like a miniature *Prelude* or *Milton*, "The Double Vision of Michael Robartes" describes an action which is a prelude to poetry.

Yeats's next pair of Greater Romantic Lyrics, "The Tower, II" and "Meditations in Time of Civil War, VII," strikes a middle ground between the personal images of dead friends in "In Memory of Major Robert Gregory" and "All Souls' Night" and the impersonal ones of inhuman extremes in "The Second Coming" and "The Double Vision of Michael Robartes." Both poems make the tower top into a symbolic outpost on the border between self and soul. Yet unlike "The Tower," discussed above, "Meditations"[17] draws its images not from past associations of the landscape but from an analogous event in history—the murder of Jacques Molay, Grand Master of the Templars, which it counterpoints with figures derived from Gustave Moreau's visionary painting "Ladies and Unicorns." They become the ingredients of one of Yeats's most moving struggles against the hatred inherent in the age and in some of his own thought. As he stands upon the tower top, images of first the troop of murderers and then the procession of ladies swim "to the mind's eye." In terms of the poem's title, the first represent "Phantoms of Hatred" and the second those "Of the Heart's Fullness." The imagination tries to counter images of hatred with those of fullness, but as even they yield to "an indifferent multitude . . . brazen hawks . . . Nothing but grip of claws," the poem modulates out of vision into its third and final section. There Yeats descends from the tower top, regrets his separation from friends and public approval, but still resignedly affirms his continued allegiance to "the half-read wisdom of daemonic images." That moment becomes all the more poignant for its frank avowal of human cost.

Although Yeats paired "The Crazed Moon" with "Coole Park, 1929" in *The Winding Stair*, he had written it in 1923, shortly after the other Greater Romantic Lyrics on *Vision* themes. Like them, it can be read in terms of Yeats's system: In a late phase, the moon shines only on moonstruck, disorganized gropers, in contrast to her exuberant children of earlier phases, who danced in order. Further, the later children grow murderous as the gyre approaches conclusion, and they long maliciously to rend whatever comes in reach. But the poem can also be read more literally, as a Greater Romantic Lyric of mental action:

> Crazed through much child-bearing
> The moon is staggering in the sky;
> Moon-struck by the despairing
> Glances of her wandering eye
> We grope, and grope in vain,
> For children born of her pain.
>
> Children dazed or dead!
> When she in all her virginal pride
> First trod on the mountain's head
> What stir ran through the countryside
> Where every foot obeyed her glance!
> What manhood led the dance!
>
> Fly-catchers of the moon,
> Our hands are blenched, our fingers seem
> But slender needles of bone;
> Blenched by that malicious dream
> They are spread wide that each
> May rend what comes in reach.   (VP 487–88)

The three stanzas reenact the familiar triple pattern, matching out-in-out with present-past-present. The speaker first describes the current state of the old moon, then creates a vision of the moon in virginal pride inspiring both passion ("stir") and order ("dance"), and finally

returns to the present with perceptions of our vain groping's goal—
malicious destruction. The landscape here is remarkably insubstantial
even for Yeats; one feels as though the speaker were charting a symbolic
romantic landscape rather than an actual scene. Polysemously, the
moon can refer to a natural object, the twenty-eight phases of A *Vision*,
historical development in clock time, or imagination withering from
exultance to despair. In his current condition, the speaker's only
triumph is to re-create past glory from memory.

Yeats transfers that theme to his favorite Irish setting in the follow-
ing poem of *The Winding Stair*, "Coole Park, 1929." The poem contrib-
utes to the book's running modern adaptation of romanticism, follow-
ing the Shelleyan tower of "Blood and the Moon" and literary history
of "The Nineteenth Century and After" and "Three Movements,"
picking up the Greater Romantic Lyric form of "The Crazed Moon,"
and anticipating romantic self-avowal in "Coole Park and Ballylee,
1931" and romantic artifice in "Byzantium." He returns to the Coole-
Ballylee region for the national ballast with which he habitually sought
to weight romanticism. The landscape's significance derives neither
from mere personal experience nor from the arbitrary mythology of A
Vision, but from its importance to actual historical figures, albeit ones
transformed by Yeats's imagination. These historical types, which in-
clude the younger Yeats himself, become quasi-objective analogues to
romantic symbols of passion and mood.

The poem opens with a conventional enough beginning for a
Greater Romantic Lyric: In a specific landscape at nightfall, the
speaker meditates on a bird's flight and even identifies the surrounding
trees as a sycamore and a lime.[18] Although the swallow may pick up the
Neoplatonic echoes[19] which Yeats associated with romanticism in
general and Shelley in particular, its overt development in the poem
follows orthodox romantic use of singing birds to symbolize artists and
their works. The ensuing portions champion freedom from oppressive
nature, which Yeats always commended in romanticism, in explicating
why the speaker fixes his eye on works constructed "in nature's spite."

With the vision of former glory in the second stanza, the speaker
reverts to the past. Noble Hyde, meditative Synge, and impetuous
Shawe-Taylor and Hugh Lane, with Yeats himself in ironic compan-
ionship, become heroic figures whose action indicates the poem's real
symbol of passion and mood, Lady Gregory herself. Her character most
rouses Yeats's intensity of vision as he moves in the third stanza from

remembering the past to creating the powerful image of swallows whirling in formation around her true north. The concluding couplet, with its off-rhyme of "lines" and "withershins" and suggestion both of gyres and of imaginative *kairos* replacing natural *chronos*, exhausts his imagination in a momentary blaze.

Superficially, the "here" of the final stanza seems to signal the close of a conventional Greater Romantic Lyric. We expect completion of normative here-there-here, out-in-out, and present-past-present movements. But Yeats plays against our vain anticipation, for "here" turns out to be placed in an imagined future. It is as if Wordsworth's "Tintern Abbey" or Coleridge's "Frost at Midnight" omitted its return to the present which separates its vision of the past from that of the future. Instead, Yeats moves directly from past to future in imagining later travelers, scholars, and poets (or perhaps the ghosts of those mentioned in stanza two) taking their stand at a ruined Coole and paying tribute to Lady Gregory. By replacing a return to self with a return to vision, Yeats shifts our attention away from the speaker and toward his overt subject. We end in contemplation of Coole rather than of Yeats's relation to it.

Yeats's adventures with the Greater Romantic Lyric show a sensibility with affinities to Shelley and Blake reworking a poetic form developed principally by Coleridge, Wordsworth, and Keats. The resultant collision exploded the original importance of nature to the form. For Yeats vision became the summoning of images and, in the highest case, active creation of them *de novo*. He pruned his natural descriptions radically, reducing them to a minimum and exploiting their national associations. This transformed his predecessors' concern with tension between mind and nature to tension between mind and images. That dialectic suited his antinomial correction of the emphasis on ideal beauty in his earlier works; through it, he could reach a poetry of insight and knowledge rather than of longing and complaint. The resultant Greater Romantic Lyrics of mental action form one branch of Yeats's mature and innovative romanticism.

PART TWO
Remaking Poets

6 Yeats's Romantic Dante

"When I was fifteen or sixteen my father had told me about Rossetti and Blake and given me their poetry to read; and once at Liverpool on my way to Sligo I had seen *Dante's Dream* in the gallery there, a picture painted when Rossetti had lost his dramatic power and today not very pleasing to me, and its colour, its people, its romantic architecture had blotted all other pictures away," recalled W. B. Yeats in his autobiography.[1] Yeats responded so deeply not to the earlier watercolor at the Tate Gallery but rather to the later oil version of *Dante's Dream at the Time of the Death of Beatrice*, Rossetti's largest picture and one of his most important. Chief among its colors were the red and gold which Yeats thought Shelley had imported from Italy for English poetry; chief among its people were the quester poet and his dead beloved, whom henceforth he might apprehend sometimes in vision but could only join permanently in death; and chief among its elements of "romantic architecture" was a winding stair spiraling upward at the extreme right. One sees how the picture blotted out all others for Yeats. Yet his reminiscence indicates more about his lifelong liaison with Dante than simply the correspondence of painterly details with his own art. Yeats consistently saw Dante as a romantic artist, whether associated with strong early Romantics like Blake or with their weaker followers like Rossetti.

If Yeats saw himself as the last romantic, he often saw Dante as the first. The tradition in which Yeats placed himself thus stretched from Dante through Blake and Shelley—the two most important of all poets to him—to his own day. Yeats mentioned Dante over ninety times in his published prose, sometimes at length, and adapted Dante's work for parts of at least ten poems, three plays, and a story. He saw Dante above all as a quest poet with whom he shared devotion to an unattainable woman, political office in a strife-torn land, exile (voluntary in Yeats's case), acceptance of an abstruse system of belief, and a host of poetic goals, not least of which was to become a character in his own work. Yet because Dante belonged to another age, did not dominate English poetic tradition, and never inspired his young Irish admirer to discipleship, Yeats could on occasion elevate him beyond even Blake and Shelley, as a rebellious son will substitute a grandfather for a father in family romance. Although he could criticize Dante too, Yeats more often made him into a foil to the high Romantics, a heroic predecessor free from their faults, which were usually those of Yeats at the time, and embodying a near-perfect achievement at which Yeats coincidentally aimed. This happened during two principal periods. In the 1890s Yeats saw Dante as the aesthetic figure of Rossetti's paintings and translations or Blake's illustrations (on which Yeats wrote a long essay), marred only by the tinge of moralism which Blake had detected. But Dante atoned for that by incorporating into his art national and folk elements, just as Yeats diligently sought to ground romanticism in his own native soil. His second period of intense interest in Dante spans the decade from composition in 1915 of *Ego Dominus Tuus*, whose title he found in Rossetti's translation of the *Vita Nuova*, to publication in 1925 of the first version of *A Vision*, where Dante appears in Yeats's own phase seventeen. But by then Yeats had grown to prize the dramatic qualities he missed in his 1921 comment on Rossetti's picture. Now Dante emerged as a poet of successful self-dramatization through mask, in contrast to the hapless Keats of *Ego Dominus Tuus*, and of acceptance of dramatic conflict in the world, in contrast to the belabored Shelley of *A Vision*. Yeats not only projected onto Dante his own great mature goal of Unity of Being but also traced the related concepts of antithetical completion and a Vision of Evil back to him. His lifelong sympathetic portrayal resulted in a figure of varied and increasing importance. After exploring the romantic origins of Yeats's interest, this essay analyzes his continual transformations of Dante into a perfected Romantic exemplifying his own poetic programs and concludes with his prime poetic adaptations of his predecessor.

Literary history sanctions Yeats's association of Dante with the Romantics, for in England the Romantics rediscovered Dante after centuries of neglect. That information surprises most modern readers, conditioned directly or indirectly by Eliot's influential description of Dante as "antiromantic."[2] Yet after Chaucer's overt allegiance, Dante's reputation began a long decline in England and reached a nadir in the early eighteenth century. By 1600 Eliot's admired Donne, for instance, spoke for many of his contemporaries when he "flung away Dant[e] the Italian a man pert enough to bee beloved & to[o] much to bee beeleeved."[3] In contrast, Milton—who became the great precursor of the Romantics and perennial bête noire of Eliot—found few sympathizers for his more favorable view of Dante. By the neoclassic period, Chesterfield provided in this as in so much else an accurate register of public taste in citing Dante as an "obscure and difficult" author who "certainly does not think clearly. . . . Though I formerly knew Italian extremely well, I could never understand him; for which reason I had done with him, fully convinced that he was not worth the pains necessary to understand him."[4] Many Augustans shared Chesterfield's censures and found Dante not merely difficult but even crabbed and scholastic. Further, Dante ran roughshod over neoclassic rules and refinements. He seemed bizarre and gothic, capable of occasional power but too often lacking design and decorum. Horace Walpole, for example, lambasted Dante with special fervor as part of a general denunciation of all epic poets but Homer: "Dante was extravagant, absurd, disgusting, in short a Methodist parson in Bedlam."[5] But by the end of the century a countermovement had already set in. If Dante was often rude and unpolished, he could also be sublime and original. The age found its favorite grotesque episode in the story of Ugolino, of which Joshua Reynolds did a famous painting in 1773, and its favorite tender one in the history of Paolo and Francesca. Blake later illustrated these two famous episodes, Shelley helped translate one of them, and they both attracted Yeats.

The romantic period transformed the perverse but pathetic Dante of the Augustans into a powerful visionary fit to rank with Milton and Shakespeare. He acquired immense prestige both for his own achievement and as an antidote to neoclassic norms. The Romantics paid repeated tribute to him: One thinks, for example, of Coleridge's 1818 lecture on Dante, Wordsworth's sonnet on Dante's seat in Florence, Byron's *Dante's Prophecy*, Keats's selection of Dante as sole text for a walking tour, Shelley's *Triumph of Life*, and the aged Blake learning Italian expressly to read Dante. For Yeats, Blake's series of illustrations and Shelley's remarks on Dante in the *Defence* (his favorite critical text) dominated all others. From both he would have learned not just praise but the dynamics of distortion, for Blake's designs embodied intermittent "correction" of Dante's legalism and Shelley's analysis a selective emphasis on Dante as a poet wholly dedicated to love.

As Dante's reputation grew so did the number of his readers, both in the original and in translation. The first full rendering of *The Divine Comedy* into English appeared only in 1802, while Cary's more influential one followed in 1814. Coleridge's praise of Cary's work in his own 1818 lecture touched off an explosion of public interest that sold a thousand copies at once, led to the first of many new editions, and eventually earned Cary a tomb in Westminster Abbey. All the great Romantics read Cary's version, as did Yeats after them, and most praised it extravagantly.[6] By 1887 a critic could observe that "from that time forward no man aiming at literary reputation thought his education complete unless he had read Dante in Cary or the original."[7] Young men aiming at such reputation in 1887 included Yeats, who knew no Italian. He read first Cary and then Charles Lancelot Shadwell for the *Comedy* (at least the two parts of it that Shadwell translated) and Dante Gabriel Rossetti for the *Vita Nuova* and lyrics. "I am no Dante scholar, and I but read him in Shadwell or in Dante Rossetti," announced Yeats in 1917.[8] To read those and other nineteenth-century translators was not to read Dante, but to read a Dante filtered through a style and diction derived from romantic practice. The Romantics shaped Yeats's view of Dante not only through their influential pronouncements but also through their impact upon a century of translation.

Nineteenth-century self-consciousness about its rediscovery of Dante and an increasing tendency to aestheticize him came together in an essay that Yeats read near the start of his career, Walter Pater's 1892 introduction to Shadwell's *Purgatory*. Here again, as in his better-known pronouncements in *The Renaissance* (which he dedicated to Shadwell) on intensity and the ecstatic moment, Pater anticipates Yeats's early position. He began by citing Voltaire's hostility as reflecting "the general unfitness of the last century in regard to the Middle Age, of whose spirit Dante is the central embodiment."[9] But Pater detected more than a mere taste for medievalism in his own generation's interest. Dante to them articulated the chief concerns of the nineteenth century itself. In particular, Dante displayed the "minuteness" of observation and fine shades of expression necessary to render not merely the external world but, more importantly, the mental phenomena that Pater calls "subjectivities." Ever since Hallam's essay on Tennyson, of course, Victorian critics had found their favorite "subjective" poets in Keats and Shelley, whose impact they rightly saw first on early Tennyson and Browning and then on Rossetti and others. To that tradition Pater tried to graft religious enthusiasm and relevance to "life": "A minute sense of the external world and its beauties, a minute sense of the phenomena of the mind, of what is beautiful and of interest there, a demand for wide and cheering outlooks in religion, for a largeness of spirit in its application to life:—these are the special points of contact between Dante and the genius of our own century." Yeats, like many of his cohorts in the Rhymers' Club of the 1890s, tended to splinter Pater's subjectivity from his social sanctions. For most of the decade Yeats lauded a perceptually sensitive Dante and lamented the religious orthodoxy and engagement with practical life which seemed to stain his subjectivity.

Inspired by Rossetti's painting of *Dante's Dream*, Yeats early assimilated the *Vita Nuova* to fin de siècle etiolations of romanticism, but until Pater's essay he thought of the *Divine Comedy*—when he bothered to think of it at all—as a remote, imposing structure showing by contrast the smallness and yet the subtlety of modern poetry. "Modern writers, the great no less than the small among them, have been heavily handicapped by being born in a lyric age, and thereby compelled for the most part to break up their inspiration into many glints and glimmers, instead of letting it burn in one steady flame," he wrote in obvious recollection of the conclusion to *The Renaissance*. "It is true that they have their compensations, for the glints and glimmers find their way into many a corner and cranny that never could be reached by the Great Light of a Divine Comedy or an Iliad."[10] Such thinking led to a hole-and-corner aestheticism, in which the modern poet refined his sensibility sheltered from the glare of his great predecessors. Yeats could not long hold that stance. Pater revealed to him that Dante, too, ranked with subjective artists, albeit marked by more rigorous religion and more direct involvement with life than the fin de siècle norm. Yeats for the rest of his life would puzzle over the relation between Dante's public system and his personal subjectivity. He at first thought that Dante's vast structures limited imagination and only later came to consider that they liberated it.

Yeats's early and derivative wave of interest in Dante crested in his essays on "William Blake and his Illustrations to the Divine Comedy" (1896) and "William Blake and the Imagination" (1897), now paired in *Ideas of Good and Evil*. Like Yeats's other major statements on Dante, these first ones contrast him with a leading romantic poet. The essay on illustrations treats Blake more sympathetically than Dante, while the later one more typically makes Dante into an ideal romantic poet. The present text of *Ideas of Good and Evil* obscures this chronological progression both by reversing the order of the essays and by dating each of them 1897; in fact "William Blake and his Illustrations" appeared a year earlier, in the *Savoy* for July, August, and September of 1896. The essay has three parts: An opening section, "His Opinions on Art," explains Blake's admiration for definite outline, minute particulars, and exuberant energy; "His Opinions on Dante" contrasts the systems of the two visionaries; and the final "The Illustrators of Dante" berates Stradanus, Genelli, Schuler, Flaxman, Signorelli, and Gustave Doré ("a noisy and demagogic art"[11]) but praises Botticelli, Giulio Clovio, the little-known Adolph Stürler, and of course Blake. Yeats had known Blake's series of 102 illustrations to the *Comedy* at least since the early nineties, when he had praised that unfinished final work in both his editions of Blake.[12]

The essay interpreted both Blake and Dante as ancestors of nine-teenth-century aesthetes. Yeats sounds like Hallam in arguing that Blake "strove to embody more subtle raptures, more elaborate intu-itions than any before him," and he imitates Pater in valuing "'the minute particulars of life,' the little fragments of space and time, which are flooded by beautiful emotion" (E&I 127, 135). The phrases de-scribe not the frenzied Blake of Yeats's maturity, who beat upon the wall till truth obeyed his call, but a Blake seen through the spectacles of late Victorian subjectivity. Yeats consigned Dante to the same camp. He disparaged those who would distinguish Blake's world from Dante's, "as if Dante's world were more than a mass of symbols of colour and form and sound which put on humanity, when they arouse some mind to an intense and romantic life that is not theirs" (E&I 141). This view reduces Dante to a source of exquisite sensory stimulation that the spectator can anthropomorphize, as Yeats liked to do in the manner of Rossetti. It also reduces the possible poetic adaptation of Dante to local effects.

Eager to preserve Dante's subjectivity, Yeats rejected his broader system under guise of comparing it to Blake's. He fleshed out Blake's scattered comments on Dante into a diabolical reading of the Italian parallel to Blake's own transformation of Milton. "Dante saw devils where I saw none," said Blake. "I see good only" (E&I 131). In Yeats's sympathetic elaboration, Dante emerged as a great poet contaminated by a philosophy of judgment and punishment which secretly derived from the absorption in worldly affairs which it sought to condemn; Dante had mistaken Satan, the true architect of his Hell, for his divinity, and in symbolizing God by the Primum Mobile he chose the symbol farthest removed from the human form divine. This diabolical reading held that "Dante, who deified law, selected its antagonist, passion, as the most important of sins," but that "Blake, who deified imaginative freedom, held 'corporeal reason' for the most accursed of things" (E&I 139). Against this it is futile to argue that Dante, as a Christian, neither deifies law nor makes passion the most important sin (indeed, in both *Inferno* and *Purgatorio* passion is the least severe sin), for Yeats does not really mean to criticize Dante. He means to convince himself that his own preoccupation with abstract system menaces his creative life as poet. He in fact shared Dante's belief in a spiritual order existing independently of man, and his salvation as artist came when he learned to use that order to free rather than fetter his own imagination.

If Yeats's essay did not advance the state of Dante scholarship, it did contribute to Dante studies in a way which unfortunately backfired upon the controversial *Savoy*. The only Blakean illustrations to the *Comedy* already available were the seven plates he had managed to engrave before his death. Along with two of those engravings—*The Circle of Thieves* and Yeats's favorite, *Paolo and Francesca*, which he wanted to use as frontispiece for *Ideas of Good and Evil*—the *Savoy* printed for the first time eight of Blake's other designs as accompaniment to the essay.[13] The reproductions both disseminated these important illustrations to an influential audience and led to the failure of the magazine. W. H. Smith and Son, the booksellers who controlled the railway stalls, objected to the frankness of the designs and refused henceforth to carry the *Savoy*. As Yeats tells the story, Smith's manager objected particularly to Blake's version of *Antaeus Setting Virgil and Dante upon the Verge of Cocytus*, which he apparently mistook for a Beardsley drawing and feared would offend young ladies (A 323). Symons as editor lamented this philistinism in his farewell to his

readers.[14] To Yeats the episode provided another sad example of the
conflict between elite art and a mass audience.

Blake did not long have the best of Dante in Yeats's prose. Yeats had
made a pass at impartiality even in the essay on illustrations to the
Comedy. Although clearly sympathetic to the diabolical reading, he
claimed to have taken Blake's side simply because Dante enjoyed so
much greater public knowledge. "By thus contrasting Blake and Dante
by the light of Blake's paradoxical wisdom, and as though there was no
important truth hung from Dante's beam of the balance, I but seek to
interpret a little-understood philosophy rather than one incorporate in
the thought and habits of Christendom," he insisted ingenuously (E&I
134). The next year Yeats redressed the balance of his second and
shorter Blake essay. The truth that weighed heaviest from Dante's
beam turned out to be the very use of material incorporate in the
thought and habits of Christendom noted a year earlier. Toward the
end of his short "William Blake and the Imagination" (1897) Yeats
invoked Dante to explain Blake's continuing inaccessibility:

> [Blake] spoke confusedly and obscurely because he spoke of
> things for whose speaking he could find no models in the
> world about him. He was a symbolist who had to invent his
> symbols; and his counties of England, with their correspon-
> dence to tribes of Israel, and his mountains and rivers, with
> their correspondence to parts of a man's body, are arbi-
> trary. . . . He was a man crying out for a mythology, and
> trying to make one because he could not find one to his
> hand. Had he been a Catholic of Dante's time he would
> have been well content with Mary and the angels; or had he
> been a scholar of our time he would have taken his sym-
> bols . . . from Norse mythology; or . . . Welsh mythol-
> ogy . . . or have gone to Ireland and chosen for his symbols
> the sacred mountains, along whose sides the peasant still
> sees enchanted fires, and the divinities which have not
> faded from the belief . . . and have been less obscure be-
> cause a traditional mythology stood on the threshold of his
> meaning. (E&I 114)

Through the example of Blake, that passage analyzes a major obsta-
cle for modern poets more acutely than it proposes a remedy. Although

Blake's symbolism owes more to tradition than Yeats allowed, he not only invented his own myth but thought that he had to in order to avoid enslavement by another man's. Yet avoiding enslavement also meant avoiding easy accessibility. So did construction of the myths of most modern poets. Pound's correlation of disparate traditions, Eliot's adaptation of Indian, Christian, and Middle Eastern fertility rites in *The Waste Land*, and even Stevens's attempt to evolve a supreme fiction all rank with Blake's mythopoetic achievement but similarly lack the ready comprehension that Dante's adaptation of Catholic myth bore for readers of his time. Yeats sought to ground his own work in Irish soil and continually claimed to have corrected romanticism by fastening it to national mythology. "I could not endure, however, an international art, picking stories and symbols where it pleased," he wrote of himself at the time of *Oisin*. "Might I not . . . create some new *Prometheus Unbound*; Patrick or Columcille, Oisin or Finn, in Prometheus' stead; and, instead of Caucasus, Cro-Patrick or Ben Bulben? Have not all races had their first unity from a mythology that marries them to rock and hill?" (A 194). But Yeats's proposed remedy works only a little better than the cosmopolitanism he detested. Even in his own time his use of Irish material caused problems even among Irish readers, most of whom learned about Oisin or Finn from recent books rather than from ongoing tradition. And Blake would not have been more accessible had he taken his symbols from Norse, Welsh, or Irish tradition. They would have caused his non-Norse readers, say, as much trouble as Yeats's Celticism has made for his non-Irish ones. Our time offers no counterpart to Dante's advantages.

Yeats's drive to anchor romanticism in Irish tradition led to his early insistence that Dante drew his Christian materials partly from folklore. His favorite example came from *Inferno* 13, whose souls imprisoned in trees he likened to native Celtic myth.[15] In a burst of assimilative enthusiasm he described Dante, along with Homer, Aeschylus, Sophocles, Shakespeare, Goethe, and Keats, as "folklorists with musical tongues" and insisted that Dante exploited folk sources "continuously." Yeats offers such parallels and claims more as literary propaganda than as scholarly proof, and in utilizing his own native folklore he usually does not mean to imitate Dante. Rather, he invokes Dante as sanction for his own enterprise. For Yeats, folklore implied not just ready-made audience but contact with vital imaginative tradition which had survived the onslaughts of European science and mechanism. "Europe belongs to Dante and the witches' sabbath, not to Newton," he affirmed later (Lett 807).

Dante had little direct impact on Yeats's early verse, but the one clear adaptation, the much-revised *The Countess Cathleen in Paradise*, follows the precept of grounding broader vision in local lore. Even the final title shows that, for Cathleen belongs to Irish legend, but the vision of Paradise to Dante. The original (1891) version of the poem sounded more like Rossetti than Dante, offering Cathleen as Blessed Damozel in its last quatrain:

> She goes down the floor of Heaven,
> Shining bright as a new lance;
> And her guides are angels seven,
> While young stars about her dance.[16]

Yeats brought the lines closer to Dante in his 1895 revision:

> With white feet of angels seven,
> Her white feet go glimmering,
> And above the deep of heaven,
> Flame on flame and wing on wing.

The vision of white angels with flame and wings in Paradise derives from *Paradiso* 31:

> Faces had they of flame, and wings of gold:
> The rest was whiter than the driven snow;
> And, as they flitted down into the flower . . .
>
> (Cary 514)

Yeats indicated his Dantesque source in a 1927 letter, where he discussed first the flames of purgatory and then Beatrice before quoting the final version of the poem—in which he likened Cathleen to a dancer—and then asking, "is there jealousy in such dancers or did Dante find them as little so as colour is of colour?" (Lett 731–32). Cathleen thus becomes a surrogate Beatrice, entering into the angelic company of the paradisal rose. The early context of the song in the play *The Countess Cathleen* supports the association, for after singing the lyric the First Spirit explains that he and his company must return to

the "rose by the seat of God, / Which is among the angelic multi-
tude,"[17] just as Dante's canto opens by describing the rose in which the
spirits abide: "In fashion, as a snow white rose, lay then / Before my
view the saintly multitude." Yeats, of course, had early known Dante's
rose of the *Paradiso*, but except for this one lyric it seems not to have
affected his own Rose poems. Besides gaelicizing Dante and following
Pater's appreciation of his subtle detail, the poem evinces Blake's
"correction" of Dante's legalism, for the Countess enters paradise
instead of an inferno because she has sold her soul to the devils out of
love for her starving dependents.

Brooding upon the hostile reception to *The Countess Cathleen* led
Yeats to his most habitual use of Dante during the decade and a half
from 1900 to 1914. Hostile nationalist critics had attacked the *Coun-
tess* and other plays for tarnishing the image of Ireland; an Irishwoman
would not, like Cathleen, sell her soul to the devil. Dante offered a
means of riposte against demands for a cardboard virtue. "The greater
portion of the *Divine Comedy* is a catalogue for the sins of Italy," wrote
Yeats in *Samhain* for 1905.[18] Imbued with Shelley's *Defence*, Yeats
thought that a poet could best shape his country by refusing passing
partisanship and instead developing national imagination. Dante had
done that. "A nation can only be created in the deepest thought of its
deepest minds. . . . They create national character," he wrote in
1910. "Goethe, Shakespeare, Dante, Homer have so created."[19]
Yeats, like Joyce, similarly wanted to forge the uncreated conscience of
his race. It was a romantic goal, and for the modern poet meant
alienation from his society. A year before describing the *Comedy* as a
catalogue of Italian vice, Yeats argued that "there never have been men
more unlike any Englishman's idea of himself than Keats or
Shelley. . . . We call certain minds creative because they are among
the moulders of their nation and are not made upon its mould" (E 158).

As he remade his mind and art during this period, Yeats more and
more came to value the interrelation of disparate emotions through a
consistent system of imagery. The molder of a nation had to organize its
psyche. He again paired Dante with a romantic writer to illustrate his
discovery:

> All art is sensuous, but when a man puts only his contempla-
> tive nature and his more vague desires into his art, the
> sensuous images through which it speaks become broken,

fleeting, uncertain, or are chosen for their distance from
general experience, and all grows unsubstantial and fantas-
tic. . . . If we are to sojourn there that world must grow
consistent with itself, emotion must be related to emotion
by a system of ordered images, as in the *Divine Comedy*. . . .
Shelley seemed to Matthew Arnold to beat his ineffectual
wings in the void, and I only made my pleasure in him
contented pleasure by massing in my imagination his recur-
ring images of towers and rivers, and caves with fountains in
them, and that one Star of his, till his world had grown solid
underfoot and consistent enough for the soul's habitation.
(E&I 293–94)

The passage reveals more than mere progress beyond an earlier concep-
tion of Dante's work as a congeries of aesthetic moments to a new
appreciation of its architectonic precision. Like much of Yeats's crit-
icism, it masks an astute self-evaluation under guise of considering
poets to whom he felt akin. The opening description of an unsubstan-
tial or fantastic world resulting from fleeting images based only on the
poet's contemplative nature and vaguer desires fits Yeats's mature con-
ception of his own early work. Although he had tried to deploy symbols
like the rose and cross, and although a scholar as erudite as Allen R.
Grossman can discern a systematic structure in the early work,[20] most
readers find a deficiency like that described above. More important,
Yeats needed to find it. He needed later to distort that early work
through heightening its defects, as he needed to distort the precursors
who inspired it, to free himself to create his own mature achievement.
The pairing here of Dante and Shelley both joins two poets whom
Yeats could use as models and implies why he became increasingly
hostile to Shelley but receptive to Dante. For just as Yeats had written
earlier "in imitation of Shelley" (A 66), so does he stand closer to him
in his manner of interrelating images. Dante had constructed his
imaginative system out of traditional Christianity, but Shelley had
massed his towers, rivers, caves, and stars from more eclectic sources.
So, too, did Yeats garner the recurrent symbols of his mature phase—
which he once identified as sun, moon, tower, mask, tree, and bird[21]—
and he could find a benevolent (because more distant) sanction in
Dante while he saw a threatening (because closer) similarity in Shelley.
    Fascination with the most important image for a poet's own charac-

ter, the mask, powered Yeats's resurgence of interest in Dante for the decade from 1915 to 1925. One of the most complete early formulations, *Ego Dominus Tuus*, makes Dante a paradigm of the poet successfully creating an appropriate mask. The title itself comes from the first commandment by way of the *Vita Nuova*, which Yeats cites in Rossetti's translation at the start of his gloss on the poem in *Per Amica Silentia Lunae* (M 326). Early in the *Vita Nuova* Love comes to Dante's chamber in a dream vision during which He speaks many things, of which "ego dominus tuus" becomes one of the few Dante can understand and the only one he records. Thomas Vance has shrewdly surmised the importance of the passage: "Dante's fatal commitment of his life to the love of Beatrice is identical with his initiation as a poet,"[22] for after this scene follows the first sonnet. But the application to Yeats lies not in the parallel, as Vance supposes, but in the contrast. For Dante's Love, as desire for the earthly Beatrice that becomes *caritas* for the heavenly Beatrice, Yeats substitutes the poet's passion for his antiself. Yeats's commitment not to his old love for Maud Gonne but to his new dialectic between artist and work initiates the new phase of his poetic career.

The poem itself centers on the contrast between Dante and Keats, from which Dante again emerges as perfected Romantic. Ille corrects Hic's naive notion by arguing that Dante created in his poetry an image of an antiself opposite to his ordinary personality:

Hic.   And yet
The chief imagination of Christendom,
Dante Alighieri, so utterly found himself
That he has made that hollow face of his
More plain to the mind's eye than any face
But that of Christ.

Ille.   And did he find himself
Or was the hunger that had made it hollow
A hunger for the apple on the bough
Most out of reach? and is that spectral image
The man that Lapo and that Guido knew?
I think he fashioned from his opposite
An image that might have been a stony face
Staring upon a Bedouin's horse-hair roof

> From doored and windowed cliff, or half upturned
> Among the coarse grass and the camel-dung.
> He set his chisel to the hardest stone.
> Being mocked by Guido for his lecherous life,
> Derided and deriding, driven out
> To climb that stair and eat that bitter bread,
> He found the unpersuadable justice, he found
> The most exalted lady loved by a man.

In contrast, Keats created not an antiself but simply a satisfied heightening of his normal character:

> Hic.   And yet
> No one denies to Keats love of the world;
> Remember his deliberate happiness.
>
> Ille.   His art is happy, but who knows his mind?
> I see a schoolboy when I think of him,
> With face and nose pressed to a sweet-shop window,
> For certainly he sank into his grave
> His senses and his heart unsatisfied,
> And made—being poor, ailing and ignorant,
> Shut out from all the luxury of the world,
> The coarse-bred son of a livery-stable keeper—
> Luxuriant song.   (VP 368–70)

This ascribes to Dante and Keats the same drive—a hunger for things of the world, represented by Dante's lechery and Keats's more generalized luxury. The difference lies in the resultant work. While Keats's luxuriant song became a substitute for the satisfactions denied him by life, Dante's severe ecstasy became antithetical to the worldly satisfaction he craved: His work incorporated the dialectic between his hollow and human selves. "All happy art seems to me that hollow image, but when its lineaments express also the poverty or the exasperation that set its maker to the work, we call it tragic art," explained Yeats. "Keats but gave us his dream of luxury; but while reading Dante, we never long escape the conflict . . ." (M 329). This interpretation catches Keats's desire for sensuous fulfillment but misses his crucial insistence upon the obliteration of ego through negative capability. It works a little better for Dante, about whom we have less biographical information, though Yeats stands on safer ground in the prose account when he yokes lust to political anger as twin motives. But the interpretation works best of all for Yeats himself, who has again performed a self-examination under cover of literary criticism. The description of Keats closely fits Yeats's own art of the nineties, that luxuriant song produced by a poet perpetually nervous about his ancestry and education, and the portrait of Dante limns the kind of poet Yeats wanted to become (and who found in Dante "my own mood between spiritual excitement, and the sexual torture" [Lett 731]). Indeed, the contrast between Keats and Dante opens by opposing "the gentle, sensitive mind" of modern aesthetes to the sterner "nonchalance of the hand" Yeats wanted to recover from past artists.

Yeats culled the information for his portrait mostly from readily accessible literary sources, principally Dante's own work,[23] but commentators have erred in ascribing his image of Dante in exile ("To climb that stair and eat that bitter bread") directly to Cacciaguida's famous description in *Paradiso* 17:

> Thou shalt prove
> How salt the savour is of other's bread;
> How hard the passage, to descend and climb
> By other's stairs.   (Cary 446)

Yeats's lines ultimately derive from Dante's, of course, but they do so by way of Rossetti's paraphrase in his poem *Dante at Verona*. Rossetti used Cacciaguida's remarks as epigraph but transformed them into Yeats's diction in two freer renderings during the poem itself:

> Of the steep stairs and bitter bread   (line 22)

and

> that bitter bread; / And . . . those stairs
>   (lines 501–2)

Yeats clearly remembered Rossetti in attaching "bitter" to "bread" and the demonstrative adjective (though plural instead of singular) to "stairs." Rossetti's poem itself dramatized the role of Dante that most fascinated Yeats, the visionary poet in exile.

Dante's life showed the penchant for solitude that Yeats ascribed to all subjective artists. Exile had forced Dante into gregarious circumstances which Yeats as public man knew well. They sprang from both poverty and politics. Just as Dante had needed to please princes and courtiers, so did Yeats contend first with the Abbey company and audiences and then with the duties of a senator and Nobel Prize winner. In 1919 and again in 1925 he cited sympathetically Dante's autobiographical remarks in the first treatise of the *Convito*: "Dante in that passage in the *Convito* which is, I think, the first passage of poignant autobiography in literary history . . . in describing his poverty and his exile counts as his chief misfortune that he has had to show himself to all Italy and so publish his human frailties that men who honoured him unknown honour him no more. Lacking means, he lacked seclusion, and he explains that men such as he should have but few and intimate friends."[24]

By 1925 the *Convito* seemed properly not the first "poignant" but the first "modern" autobiography. It presented the earliest self-conscious artist of the modern gyre, whose psyche operated in terms of the dialectic of will and antithetical mask; by impressing that dialectic upon an abstract system, he achieved in the *Divine Comedy* the first modern victory of personality. Such a poet found his artistic mask in the passionate quester who stood apart from society. As man he sought to retire from partisan rancor to philosophic solitude. Yeats particularly approved Dante's **refusal** of a tainted Florentine pardon in the Ninth Epistle, from which he twice quoted to his own correspondents: "Cannot I anywhere look upon the stars and think the sweet thoughts of philosophy?" (Lett 849, 882).

Yeats's own sweet thoughts of philosophy matured into *A Vision*, which contains the last of his major discussions contrasting Dante to a Romantic. The entire work has a Dantesque side. In translating the *Comedy* Cary had chosen *The Vision* as title, with *Hell, Purgatory, and Paradise of Dante Alighieri* as subtitle. More important, Yeats structured his work around an abstract system almost as geometric as Dante's, and he, too, selected historical personages to exemplify its classifications. He hoped that his esoteric system would free his imagination as he thought that medieval Christianity had freed Dante's. "I wished for a system of thought that would leave my imagination free to create as it chose and yet make all that it created, or could create, part of the one history, and that the soul's," he wrote in his original dedication. "The

Greeks certainly had such a system, and Dante—though Boccaccio thought him a bitter partisan and therefore a modern abstract man— and I think no man since" (1925V, xi). Most important of all, Yeats ascribed the highest goal of his system—the Unity of Being resulting from the antithetical mask's capacity to unite us to our true selves—to Dante: "the self so sought is that Unity of Being compared by Dante in the *Convito* to that of 'a perfectly proportioned human body'" (V 82). As scholars have realized despite Yeats's persistent assertions,[25] Dante does not make such a comparison there. Why Yeats should thus repeatedly err in citing a source for one of his principal doctrines remains a mystery, but I should like to suggest that he may have faultily remembered two passages from the Third Treatise, which in an 1887 translation ran: "Man is the most wonderful, considering how in one form the Divine Power joined three natures; and in such a form how subtly harmonized his body must be. It is organized for all his distinct powers; wherefore, because of the great concord there must be, among so many organs, to secure their perfect response to each other" and "the beauty of the body is the result of its members in proportion as they are fitly ordered. . . ."[26] Yeat's phantom translation accords well with both those passages and the general tenor of the *Convito*, and his mistaken lineage for his cherished concept signifies less than does his obvious desire to claim a Dantesque ancestry for it.

The habit of contrasting Dante with a romantic poet as alternate self-images culminated in the crucial formulation of phase seventeen in *A Vision*, the same phase to which Yeats privately assigned himself. The 1925 text used Dante and Shelley as sole examples (the brief paragraph on Landor was added for the 1937 revision). Yeats calls the man of this phase *Daimonic* because he can most easily attain Unity of Being. The *Daimonic* man does that by finding a true mask of simplification through intensity, which allows his creative imagination to forge an Image of desire in defiance of the inevitable loss which constitutes his fate. As Yeats explains, "This *Mask* may represent intellectual or sexual passion; seem some Ahasuerus or Athanase; be the gaunt Dante of the *Divine Comedy*; its corresponding Image may be Shelley's Venus Urania, Dante's Beatrice, or even the Great Yellow Rose of the Paradiso" (V 141). This illuminates a genuine if obvious affinity between Dante and Shelley, who admired him; the corresponding mask for Yeats would be the lover in his early verse and the towered philosopher of his later work. But the investigation goes increasingly awry in contrasting the relation between the life and art of the two poets. Yeats lambastes Shelley for inability to "see anything that opposes him as it really is": Shelley's millenarian hopes for the future of mankind constituted a false image for the mask and thus led him into caricatures of evil, mental instability, vague and cloudy art, and automatonism rather than poetic invention. I have argued elsewhere that these strictures so clash with both the skeptical Shelley and with Yeats's earlier and more accurate views on him that they become intelligible only as an attempt to throw off the poet who had "shaped my life"[27] and to emerge into artistic independence. The critique fits Yeats's own work of the 1890s better than it does Shelley's. Correspondingly, the portrait of Dante, while more accurate historically, offers principally a self-image of Yeats as he wished to become:

> Dante, who lamented his exile as of all possible things the worst for such as he, and sighed for his lost solitude, and yet could never keep from politics, was, according to a contemporary, such a partisan, that if a child, or a woman, spoke against his party he would pelt this child or woman with stones. Yet Dante, having attained, as poet, to Unity of Being, as poet saw all things set in order, had an intellect that served the *Mask* alone, that compelled even those things that opposed it to serve, and was content to see both good and evil. . . . Dante suffering injustice and the loss of Beatrice, found divine justice and the heavenly Beatrice, but the justice of *Prometheus Unbound* is a vague propagandist emotion and the women that await its coming are but clouds. (V 143–44)

While truer to its overt subject than the remarks on Shelley, this account epitomizes the poetic goals of the mature Yeats. He longed for a Unity of Being to render both good and evil convincingly rather than to produce the vague emotion and cloudy women he had grown to suspect in his early work. We have only to remember incidents like Dante's pleasure in Filippo Argenti's suffering in *Inferno* 8 or his abuse of Bocca degli Abbati in *Inferno* 32 to see that Yeats subtly distorts Dante's view of evil. Not only does the entire *Comedy* share a structure which condemns evil, but the *Inferno* shows in detail the replacement of Dante's initial tears and sympathy for the inmates of Hell by a sterner moralism. Yeats overstates his case in developing his true contention that Dante's view of both good and evil carries conviction. Yeats's phrase "content to see" applies better to the mature work he was then writing or would write, to *The Gyres* for example, in which acceptance on occasion degenerates into indifference or acquiescence.

Often Yeats used the notion of a Vision of Evil to compare Dante with other writers. He capitalized the phrase in *A Vision* and elsewhere to indicate that he meant not a mere vision of evil but rather a vision of both good and evil informing "the world as a continual conflict" (V 144). Need to divorce himself from his chief precursors led to continual misperception that the Romantics, like Shelley, lacked such a quality. But two writers to whom he also liked to compare Dante had it— Villon and Balzac. By accurately perceiving evil, both enabled them-selves to detect an actual rather than imaginary good as well. They avoided the pitfalls of false optimism. "Had not Dante and Villon understood that their fate wrecked what life could not rebuild, had they lacked their Vision of Evil, had they cherished any species of false optimism, they could but have found a false beauty," concluded Yeats (A 273).[28] So, too, would have Balzac, "the only modern mind which has made a synthesis comparable to that of Dante" (E 269). The *Comédie humaine* had closed a countermovement to the *Divine Comedy* (E&I 468), and Yeats saw his own work as heralding a return to Europe "upon its knees" before the supernatural. The Vision of Evil became a sort of litmus paper for determining whether a writer had achieved Unity of Being in his work. Poets like Dante or Shakespeare "sought no impossible perfection" either in the world or in their lives but only in their own artifice (M 333). The intellect of man was forced to choose.

Yeats's increasingly unfavorable comparisons of the Romantics to Dante do not imply the same attitude as do those of T. S. Eliot. Writing often from a militant antiromanticism, Eliot discerned in Dante the order, morality, and maturity that he thought Romantics would forever lack. In contrast, Yeats generally wrote from a proroman-tic position and saw Dante as a sort of perfected Romantic realizing the Romantics' goals while avoiding their supposed failures in execution. Portions of his literary criticism became a disguised psychomachia, with Dante as exemplar of what Yeats wanted to become and the Romantics of what he feared he had been. The resultant poetry owes less to Dante than does that of Eliot or Pound. Although Dante functions chiefly in Yeats's critical speculations, he did affect some of the creative work, as we have already seen. Rather than rehearse the parallels,[29] I should like instead to focus on the two most important cases, *The Second Coming* and *Byzantium*, to show Yeats's *difference* from Dante before concluding with analysis of his one sustained effort at modern Dantesque composition, *Cuchulain Comforted.*

The Second Coming (VP 401) projects into poetry the prose penchant for linking Dante with the Romantics. Its principal literary allusions systematically reverse their sources. Just as the famous lines "The best lack all conviction, while the worst / Are full of passionate intensity" counter the Last Fury's speech in act one of *Prometheus Unbound* and the phrase "stony sleep" plays against Blake's usage in *The Book of Urizen,* so do the opening lines

> Turning and turning in the widening gyre
> The falcon cannot hear the falconer

both echo and revise the description of Geryon at the end of *Inferno* 17:

> As falcon, that hath long been on the wing,
> But lure nor bird hath seen, while in despair
> The falconer cries, "Ah me! thou stoop'st to earth,"
> Wearied descends, whence nimbly he arose
> In many an airy wheel, and lighting sits
> At distance from his lord in angry mood . . .
>
> (Cary 88–89)

Not only does Geryon's flight trace a gyre, but his human head and animal body recall the shape of Yeats's rough beast. The simile of a falcon refusing the command of his master particularly suits an image of fraud like Geryon, who shuttles between the circle of the violent and the *malebolge* of the fraudulent and malicious. Yeats carries over these associations into a view of history which radically opposes Dante's own. *The Second Coming* suggests the Christian scheme of history even in its title. Yet it replaces the meaningful and finite span of that history with an endless and meaningless succession of cycles: The "second" coming could just as well be the "nth," and is in fact the third implied by the poem. The wit of Yeats's allusion lies in using a metaphor from one of the great Christian achievements of order to describe a disorder inaugurating a new historical phase which will reverse that of Christian civilization itself. Christianity is a truth for Dante, but a source of metaphors for Yeats.[30]

The use of Dantesque devices which reveal Yeats's distance from his predecessor recurs in *Byzantium*. Not only does the speaker's uncertainty about whether he confronts "an image, man or shade" recall Dante's confusion about whether Virgil be "shade, or certain man" in *Inferno* 1, but in earlier drafts the mummy functioned as a Virgil-like guide to the speaker.[31] The flames constitute the chief Dantesque echo in the final version. They recall in several ways the flames and fire of *Purgatory* 25–27, whose presence burns even clearer in the prose sketch:

> tall flames wind and unwind
> And in the flames dance spirits, by that their agony made pure
> And though they are all folded up in flame
> It cannot singe a sleeve.

Rather than unravel the details in sources, I mean instead to emphasize two distinctions between Yeats's polysemous symbolism and that of Dante. First, except for the "texts for exposition" of *A Vision*, Yeats's practice seldom depends for interpretation on a preexistent and homogenous body of doctrine that he can count on readers knowing or on a symbolic sense (as opposed to the particular meaning) that he can count on them to expect. As Dante explains in the letter to Can Grande, or in the opening of the *Convito*, his work follows the four recognized senses of medieval literature, usually referred to as the literal and the three general allegorical senses of tropological (pertaining to the individual), anagogical (pertaining to the afterlife), and formally allegorical (pertaining to Christ or the Church). Dante illustrates these by the famous example of the exodus from Egypt, but we could just as easily use the fires of his own Purgatory, which at once literally burn, tropologically show the purification of the soul from lust, anagogically the progression from body to spirit in the afterlife, and allegorically the redemption through Christ. No such scheme fits Yeats's symbolism. He draws from diverse and often philosophically contradictory sources and elaborates his meaning in senses developed by the poem itself rather than standing apart from it. Thus, the fires of *Byzantium* pertain at least both to purification after death and to artistic creativity, but the poem itself must define those senses rather than operate in terms of the reader's inherent expectation of them. Second, elevation of artistic process itself as a primary subject for the symbolism divides this poem from Dante. Dante, of course, often refers to his art and its difficulties, but concentration on creative aesthetic process as both subject and figurative sense seems a distinctively postromantic phenomenon, which Yeats shares with many other modern poets.

Deepening steadily throughout his literary career, Yeats's fascination with Dante culminated in a poem finished just two weeks before his death, *Cuchulain Comforted*. In frankly adapting Dante to the needs of a contemporary poet, that lyric forms a fit analogue to the stunning utilizations of Dante in the last major poem by Yeats's idol Shelley, *The Triumph of Life*, and by his rival Eliot, *Little Gidding*. Here is Yeats:

A man that had six mortal wounds, a man
Violent and famous, strode among the dead;
Eyes stared out of the branches and were gone.

Then certain Shrouds that muttered head to head
Came and were gone. He leant upon a tree
As though to meditate on wounds and blood.

A Shroud that seemed to have authority
Among those bird-like things came, and let fall
A bundle of linen. Shrouds by two and three

Came creeping up because the man was still.
And thereupon that linen-carrier said:
"Your life can grow much sweeter if you will

"Obey our ancient rule and make a shroud;
Mainly because of what we only know
The rattle of those arms makes us afraid.

"We thread the needles' eyes, and all we do
All must together do." That done, the man
Took up the nearest and began to sew.

"Now must we sing and sing the best we can,
But first you must be told our character:
Convicted cowards all, by kindred slain,

"Or driven from home and left to die in fear."
They sang, but had nor human tunes nor words,
Though all was done in common as before;

They had changed their throats and had the throats of birds.
(VP 634–35)

This recalls Dante not only in its terza rima but also in its subject and setting, the fate of a famous personage in the afterlife. Its twenty-five lines seem a portion of a canto from the *Comedy*. The resemblance extends even to particulars. F. A. C. Wilson has suggested the appropriate similarity of this setting to the Valley of Negligent Rulers in *Purgatory* 7–8, while T. R. Henn first noticed the parallel between Yeats's shades, who "thread the needles' eyes," and those of the sodomites who gaze "As an old tailor at his needle's eye" (Cary 74) in *Inferno* 15.[32]

Even in this most Dantesque of his poems Yeats shows a distance. The tailor image, in Dante's poem a sign of the impaired perception of the squinting sodomites in contrast to the clearer sight of Virgil and Dante, becomes in Yeats's a neutral or even positive activity of the cowards, which Cuchulain must imitate. The poem itself defines the range of application of its symbolism, with a slight assist from the eschatology of *A Vision* (Cuchulain appears to be in the state there known as the Shiftings, in which a man's nature "is reversed" [V 231]). Further *Cuchulain Comforted* lacks the full structural support of the *Comedy*, in which Dante's placement of an episode itself directs exegesis. Yeats's lyric counterpart to the architectonics of epic must rely as best it can on reflections from other Cuchulain works, related imagery elsewhere—for instance, the bird and singing school of *Byzantium*—and its placement within the volume. Scholars have increasingly realized the thematic importance of Yeats's arrangement of poems within each book. In this case his manuscript list, discovered only after the present arrangement had been set posthumously, indicates that *Cuchulain Comforted* would have come fourth in a volume moving from the supernatural determinism and escape of *Under Ben Bulben* to the choice for reimmersion in experience of *The Circus Animals' Desertion*.[33] Even Cuchulain's acceptance of his new role in the poem prepares for that movement in ratifying by implication his "violent and famous" life on earth. In this respect Yeats's poem inverts the relation between life and death that would shortly inform the only comparable modern work, the Dantesque passage in part two of *Little Gidding*. Whereas Eliot presents a bleak picture of natural senescence in implied contrast to supernatural salvation hereafter, Yeats projects a melancholy but acquiescent view of the afterlife which exalts by contrast Cuchulain's heroic life on earth.

In his crucial late tribute to Dante, Yeats himself emerges as the perfected romantic poet of his prose criticism. First, he has grounded his vision securely in Irish lore. The figure of Cuchulain carries the national particularity for which Yeats praised Dante in contrast to Blake. Second, he adopts the dialectic of the antiself which he found lacking in Keats. Not only does Cuchulain himself form a mask for Yeats, but he also here turns into his own antiself by joining the gregarious cowards instead of remaining a solitary hero. And finally, the poem displays the Vision of Evil which Yeats excoriated Shelley for lacking. Acceptance permeates the poem, as both Yeats and his hero accept the ignoble end of the noble warrior as a necessary working out of destiny. Cuchulain's willing submission strengthens both the sorrow of his present lot and the grandeur of his former state. Yeats as author at last saw all things set in order. He could now boast even more truly than he had in *The Tower:*

> I have prepared my peace
> With learned Italian things.

7 The Making of Yeats's Spenser

W hen W. B. Yeats recalled the origins of his literary career in *Reveries over Childhood and Youth*, his impulse toward mythic autobiography happily corresponded with accuracy: "I had begun to write poetry in imitation of Shelley and of Edmund Spenser, play after play—for my father exalted dramatic poetry above all other kinds—and I invented fantastic and incoherent plots."[1] As that linkage suggests, Yeats's Spenser was always a Romantic, as were the other poets into whose company Yeats sought admission as a brother.[2] Indeed, except for Shelley and Blake, Spenser influenced Yeats perhaps more than did any other English precursor. His impact extended from the plots of Yeats's early verse of the 1880s through the symbolism of the Rose poems of the 1890s to climax in the imagery and themes of some of the great mature lyrics on Lady Gregory and her son Robert. Yeats at first sought simply to imitate Spenser, then to project onto him conflicts from his own career, and finally to adapt Spenser's stance toward aristocratic patrons for his own uses. In so doing he continually revised his image of a romantic Spenser, first from a poet of fantastic pastoral to one of intense vision of beauty and then from a self-divided prophet to an impassioned lamenter of necessary defeats by time and death. Throughout, Yeats persistently paired the Renaissance poet with his romantic admirers Shelley, Keats, or Blake both in published works and in private manuscripts and marginalia, particularly those connected with his 1906 edition of Spenser.

The period of emulation began with several unpublished early plays and with a long, unpublished narrative poem in Spenserian stanzas on the adventures of a medieval knight. The poem struggles confusedly to fulfill the avowal of "Sad love and change" rather than "rime empassioned of envenomed years / Or the embattled earth" in its first and only published stanza.[3] Along the way it mixes Greek, Romance, and Norse elements in the sort of pastoral potpourri that Yeats derived from Keats's and Shelley's own redactions of Spenser. The plot is at once "fantastic and incoherent" and yet curiously anticipatory of Yeats's later preoccupations, as a summary will make clear. Like the first hero of Spenser's epic, Yeats's Sir Roland wears a red cross. Singing "a song forlorn about a lady fair / . . . / In iron Norway" (stanza 4), he enters the valley of Lethe, where he encounters another knight. The second knight, "Olaf the Hero dane" (stanza 21), tells of blessedly ruling a peaceful country until a mysterious figure sang him a song about the fair maid Ingeborg in the visionary land of unfading asphodel. Olaf then set out to seek for her by ship with a picked crew, all of whom died and left him still wandering in hopeless quest, upon which Roland seems to join him as the fragment ends. (There are scattered other stanzas which may also belong to the poem, for example those on the Spenserian figures Sansloy and Sansfoy.) Memories of *Alastor*, *Endymion*, and *Rime of the Ancient Mariner* obviously jostle with elements of *The Faerie Queene* in this early, imitative work. Yet the poem does contain the solitary quest for a visionary woman so important in Yeats's writing over the following two decades.

That theme became more prominent in *The Island of Statues*, Yeats's first major published work (1885) and one more coherent if not less fantastic than the previous unpublished dramas. In *Reveries* he would label it "an Arcadian play in imitation of Edmund Spenser" (Au 92). Imitative elements included characters like the Enchantress and the singing shepherds Colin and Thernot (or Thenot, as Yeats sometimes wrote in the drafts, after the Colin and Thenot of *The Shepherd's Calender*),[4] pastoral settings like Arcadia and the enchanted island, and the rich mellifluence of the verse. The plot itself hinged on the noble youth Almintor's quest for the magic flower to win Naschina and its ambivalent resolution, for which Yeats utilized such Spenserian devices as the magic boat that ferries first Almintor and then Naschina across the lake to the island.

The Spenserian impact survived even the sea change of Yeats's conversion to Irish materials during the second half of the 1880s. Yeats derived *The Wanderings of Oisin*, for example, primarily from translations of Gaelic originals, yet the result harmonizes with his earlier Spenserian interests. Oisin's encounter with an enchantress, journey to the islands of fairyland, and marvellous adventures all recall aspects of *The Faerie Queene* as well as the Gaelic mythology, as does some of the language. The description of Oisin's speech ("And drops of honey are his words") echoes that of Belphoebe's ("sweet words, like dropping honny");[5] in this context, Yeats's approach to Renaissance spelling in the manuscript draft, "honney,"[6] indicates more than just his often wayward orthography. Affinities to Spenserian romance help explain why this particular Gaelic story should have appealed to him so strongly.

The early but still superficial emulation of Spenserian questing deepened in the 1890s, when Yeats came to appreciate the Neoplatonic elements in *Fowre Hymns* and elsewhere. The proper object of the Spenserian and Shelleyan plots should have been Intellectual Beauty. In devising his own Rose lyrics around that theme, Yeats looked back to the hymns as much as to the narratives of Shelley and Spenser for literary precedent. Even thirty years later he could find only one distinction between his work and theirs: "I notice upon reading these poems for the first time for several years that the quality symbolised as The Rose differs from the Intellectual Beauty of Shelley and of Spenser in that I have imagined it as suffering with man and not as something pursued and seen from afar" (VP 842). That distinction, as much invented as real, parallels Yeats's desire to move downward upon life after the 1890s. The Rose poems both close and make coherent his period of early devotion.

Yeats's edition of *Poems of Spenser* (1906) for the Golden Poets series marks the middle phase of his interest. The project arose somewhat haphazardly. As he wrote to Lady Gregory in January 1902, "I have had a letter from an Edinburgh publisher asking me to edit a book of selections from Spenser for £ 35. It is good pay and I am writing to ask when it will be wanted. I may do it if I have not to do it at once. I have a good deal to say about Spenser but tremble at the thought of reading his six books."[7] Yeats's trembling changed to delight as he made his way through the six books of *The Faerie Queene*. A year later he had finished his task, though the Edinburgh firm of T. C. & E. C. Jack waited three more years to publish the resultant volume. In it Yeats eschewed representation as a principle of selection and instead chose "only those passages from Spenser that I want to remember and carry about with me."[8] The extracts thus offer a fair map of the parts of Spenser that mattered most to Yeats. He began with "An Hymne of Heavenly Beautie," included *Epithalamion* with extracts from *The Teares of the Muses, Ruines of Time,* and *The Shepherd's Calender,* and cited a few other passages on love, shepherds, or old age. From *The Faerie Queene* he excerpted his favorite sections, including the islands of Phaedria and Acrasia, the Garden of Adonis, and the vision of Scudamour. With perhaps the exception of the strong, elegiac lament for the Earl of Leicester, the passages reflect the aspects of Spenser that underlay Yeats's early adaptations.

The texts themselves and some of the notes for Yeats's edition derive from the controversial J. Payne Collier's five-volume *Works of Edmund Spenser* (London: Bell, 1862), which Lady Gregory presented to him. The unpublished but still surviving marginalia to these volumes both reveal Yeats's mind at work as he labored over the edition and provide an intimate glimpse of the way he reacted to Spenser.[9] Sometimes the marginalia simply reveal that charming side of Yeats which he so rigorously excised from his public persona. For instance, worrying over how much of Book 2, Canto 12, of *The Faerie Queene* the publishers will let him include, he finally decides, "give all canto 12 It is most beautiful" (II, 334). Again, faced with the exasperating complexities of *Muiopotmos,* he replaces a simple question mark with an increasingly desperate series of questions: "Is this poem alegorical. Is it mis Earthly ?talent against divine. reason against instinct. Calculation against genius or what?" (IV, 474). More often, the marginalia reveal three of his chief preoccupations as he read through Spenser's verse—its connection to Ireland, its exaltation of Venus or Intellectual Beauty, and its relation to romantic poetry. Yeats noted, for example, the comparison of the stones of Alma's castle to Irish marble as the "first sign of Irish influence" (II, 247). He delighted in drawing the astrological sign for Venus [♀] in the margin next to references to the goddess, star, or any other figure he could associate with Intellectual Beauty, and he often threw in the signs for Mars, Earth, and Sun as well. But most often, passages in Spenser reminded him of favorite lines of romantic poetry. These deserve a closer look.

Comparisons to romantic poets cluster most frequently in Books 2 and 3 of *The Faerie Queene,* where Yeats paused to jot comments in the margins six times. All concern Shelley, Blake, or Keats. In Book 2 he compares the magic boat in which Phaedria ferries Cymochles over the Idle Lake to the wandering island with "Shelley's boats," perhaps in particular the self-propelled shallop of *Alastor* or the enchanted craft in *The Witch of Atlas* (II, 175). In Book 3 the conception of Belphoebe and Amoret by sunrays which impregnate their supernatural mother resting in rural solitude makes him recall the analogous circumstances of the Witch of Atlas's birth (II, 447). Similarly, Spenser's witch creating the False Florimel out of snow two cantos later suggests to Yeats the hermaphroditic "figure of snow" molded by Shelley's witch to be her companion (II, 486). The two Blake references are more general. When Satyrane encounters the giantess Argante riding with a doleful squire "bounded hand and foote with cords of wire," Yeats remembers that "Blake has chords or nets of wire," as in "The Golden Net"; and Spenser's likening to a discolored snake of the golden threads of the arras in Busyrane's castle where Scudamour languishes reminds Yeats of "Blake's serpent" (II, 477, and III, 52). Those correlations are both supple and acute, striking us with a fine surprise. But none shows Yeats's powers of connection and revision so well as the sole reference to Keats.

When Phaedria conducts Cymochles across the Idle Lake to the island, Spenser writes:

Thus when shee had his eyes and sences fed
With false delights, and fild with pleasures vayn,
Into a shady dale she soft him led,
And layd him downe upon a grassy playn;
And her sweete selfe without dread or disdayn
She sett beside, laying his head disarmd
In her loose lap, it softly to sustayn,
Where soone he slumbered fearing not be harmd:
The whils with a love lay she thus him sweetly charmd.

Coming across this passage, Yeats notes in the margin, "La Belle Dame Sans Merci" (II, 178). The parallels leap out at once: In both poems a supernatural lady misleads a fallible human quester into a hopeless love, entices him to a secluded bower, and charms him asleep with a love song, from which he will awaken disillusioned. Yet the differences rate equal attention. The brother of the fiery Pyrochles, Cymochles represents anger; he consorts with Acrasia, who presides over the sensual Bower of Bliss; and he eventually is killed by Arthur while despoiling the knight of Temperance, Guyon. His story may suggest broad psychological or imaginative truth, but it also occupies a clear place in the governing Christian allegory of the poem. Keats's knight carries no such Christian connotations. Instead, he stands as a symbol of a mistaken questing for an imaginary ideal wholly separate from the actual. In linking the two stories, Yeats typically ignores Spenser's Christian allegory to focus on elements compatible with a romantic parable of imaginative questing.

The introduction to *Poems of Spenser* writes large the dichotomies of the marginalia. Yeats subsumed the essay into his critical canon by reprinting it under the title "Edmund Spenser" in *The Cutting of an Agate*. Displaying his characteristic fondness for antinomies, he there saw Spenser as divided between a positive, poetically symbolic, aristocratic, and Anglo-French delight in the senses and a negative, prosaically allegorical, middle-class, and Anglo-Saxon allegiance to the emerging State. These antitheses allowed him to admire the romantic and poetic side of Spenser even while confessing the harshness of *View of the Present State of Ireland,* which troubled his nationalist sympathies. The positive qualities had engendered the later, romantic poetry of Keats, Shelley, and Blake, whose names dot the essay as they do the marginalia. But even as the Romantics elaborated on Spenser more subtly and more intellectually, they lost the sureness of personal instinct that distinguishes his best work. The result was a retreat from the world and "disintegration of the personal instincts which has given to modern poetry its deep colour for colour's sake, its overflowing pattern, its background of decorative landscape, and its insubordination of detail" (E&I 357). The problem extended even to versification: One had only to compare a stanza from Shelley's *Laon and Cythna* with Spenser's own cadences to conclude that "the rhythm is varied and troubled, and the lines, which are in Spenser like bars of gold thrown ringing one upon another, are broken capriciously. . . . It is bound together by the vaguest suggestion" (E&I 379).

Those defects of excessive attention to detail, troubled rhythms, and vague suggestion sound suspiciously like Yeats's own criticisms of his own early poetry. Indeed, the entire essay—written as Yeats began his movement downward upon life after the aestheticism of the 1890s—

reads like a projection of the dangers that he himself feared as he reoriented his own poetry. Would he, like Spenser, forsake the "self-exciting, self-appeasing soul" through trying "to be of his time, or rather of the time that was all but at hand," or would he be able to transform that time "in the mythology of his imagination"? (E&I 370, 358). When Yeats observes "that conflict between the aesthetic and moral interests that was to run through wellnigh all his [Spenser's] works" (E&I 360), we may recall the conflict between aesthetic and occult ones that pervades his own. Just as Yeats's description of the Romantics recapitulates his own recent poetic experience, so does his conception of Spenser's misadventures with Puritan Christianity prefigure the form his own struggles with occult dogmas would henceforth take. "Texts for exposition" were his analogue to Spenserian allegory, and he came to regret even the few that he eventually wrote.

After the Spenser edition Yeats approached his sometime model only with care, as though too close contact with the inspirer of his early islands and escapist paradises would weaken the new strength he sought for his own poetry. But he did turn to Spenser for one of his strongest achievements, the powerful elegiac laments for a lost aristocratic tradition. Much influenced by Castiglione's concept of the courtier, Yeats had included in his edition an excerpt from *Mother Hubbard's Tale*, which was itself a redaction of Castiglione's precepts.[10] With the death of Robert Gregory, Yeats drew upon Spenser to enrich his own allegiance to the Gregory family, particularly in the elegiac mode. Spenser's laments for Sidney in *Astrophel* and for the Earl of Leicester in *The Ruines of Time* lie behind Yeats's own commemorative efforts. In a letter to Lady Gregory on 22 February 1918 he described his first elegy for her son Robert, "Shepherd and Goatherd," as "in manner like one that Spenser wrote for Sir Philip Sidney" (L 646). The likeness included pastoral shepherds, lament for a young aristocrat dead in a foreign war, and a vision of his continued life as much Neoplatonic or pagan as Christian. The subsequent and more powerful "In Memory of Major Robert Gregory" differs in design and form but still refers to Robert (the soldier, scholar, horseman, and painter) as "Our Sidney and our perfect man" (VP 325).

In the very late "The Municipal Gallery Revisited" (1937) Yeats fittingly turned to Spenser for the last time in a major way, bidding goodbye as much to the progenitor of his favorite literary images as to the painters and friends who had inspired the artistic and personal ones he so loved. Even in the edition of thirty years before he had noticed that Spenser's lament for the Earl of Leicester in *The Ruines of Time* belonged with those passages on men that "seem to express more of personal joy and sorrow than those about women" in his poetry (E&I 359). For Yeats, of course, that situation was often reversed. In his own poem he laments the demise of Lady Gregory's Coole Park in an explicit recollection of the Leicester passage:

> And now that end has come I have not wept;
> No fox can foul the lair the badger swept—
>
> (An image out of Spenser and the common tongue)
>   (VP 603).

Those lines carry the full weight both of Yeats's lifelong encounter with Spenser and of his mature revision of the romantic tradition through which he viewed his great predecessor. Most overtly, the echo revises Spenser's image, which Yeats had glossed in his 1906 edition as: "At the end of a long beautiful passage he laments that unworthy men should be in the dead Earl's place, and compares them to the fox—an unclean feeder—hiding in the lair 'the badger swept'" (E&I 359–60). "The Municipal Gallery Revisited" keeps the Spenserian sense but explicitly reverses its application by barring the fox from defiling its heritage. It doubtless pleased Yeats that Spenser had in mind his enemy Lord Burleigh, whose Irish policy had been so harsh. Yet the allusion here carries far more than mere national resentment; it also embodies Yeats's claim to have corrected romanticism by fastening it to a national landscape, in this case Coole Park. Among other things, "The Municipal Gallery Revisited" is a great poem of romantic meditation on the dialectics of image and memory, assimilated to an Irish context. Yeats's nationalist use of that context contrasts to Spenser's co-option of it in the service of English imperialism as well as to the English or Continental attachments Yeats saw in romantic poetry. At the same time, the poem's placement in its volume—second from the end, just before "Are You Content?"—reverses Yeats's stony renunciation of human ties and sympathy in the cyclic patterns of the opening poem "The Gyres" ("What matter?") in favor of the human and humane attachments of these lines:

And I am in despair that time may bring
Approved patterns of women or of men
But not that selfsame excellence again.
. . . .
Think where man's glory most begins and ends,
And say my glory was I had such friends.

The poem thus marshals Yeats's mature thought and skill in the service of a revised romanticism which gives his later work its memorable strength. The question and answer he scrawled on a sheet of Lady Gregory's own notepaper could just as well be applied to his own work: "Why gentle Spenser? He is rather powerful than gentle."[11]

8 Last Romantic or Last Victorian: Yeats, Tennyson, and Browning

To consider the affinity of Yeats—or any other twentieth-century poet—to the Victorians contradicts a fundamental dogma of modernist poetics. We say, did not modernism arise in protest against a flaccid Victorian theory and practice of the poetic art? Didn't verbosity, abstraction, and insincerity continually undermine the palace of art in the nineteenth century? How absurd in our ears would Yeats have sounded had he declared in "Coole Park and Ballylee, 1931" that "We were the last Victorians—chose for theme / Traditional sanctity and loveliness . . . whatever most can bless / The mind of man or elevate a rhyme."[1] Yet even the content of that overtly romantic avowal (choosing "traditional sanctity and loveliness"), as well as its diction ("Bless the mind of man"), suggests how much more Yeats owed to the Victorian era than simply spending the first thirty-six years of life in it. Ordinarily, we do not see this because the Victorians play the same role in the politics of poetic history now that the Romantics did in the early 1950s—the disloyal opposition. Both Victorian poetry itself and its role in English literary history await that transvaluation which romanticism has undergone in the last quarter century.[2] The desire to show how such a change in context might modify our view of Yeats makes me here scant his established linkage with a Victorian countertradition running from Hallam's redaction of romanticism through Rossetti, Pater, and Morris to the aesthetes of the Rhymers' Club. Instead, while returning to the crucial impact of Hallam's essay on Yeats, I intend to consider his uneasy relationship to the two poets whom he rightly judged chief among the Victorians—Tennyson and Browning. They did not, of course, displace the Romantics Blake and Shelley as Yeats's prime poetic predecessors, but they did alert him to both models and menaces in his own poetic development. For Tennyson and Browning were the first postromantic poets, the first to identify themselves fully with the romantic enterprise in their youths and then to achieve their poetic maturity through ambivalent reaction against it, just as Yeats himself would later do. Yeats was in nothing so Victorian as in his relation to romanticism.

Modernist critical antipathy toward Victorianism derives partly from too credulous acceptance of pronouncements by the modern masters themselves. Those militant manifestos warrant more wariness than they often receive. As T. S. Eliot confessed with some embarrassment in 1942,

> The critical writings of poets . . . owe a great deal of their interest to the fact that the poet, at the back of his mind, if not as his ostensible purpose, is always trying to defend the kind of poetry he is writing, or to formulate the kind that he wants to write. Especially when he is young, and actively engaged in battling for the kind of poetry which he prac-tises . . . He is not so much a judge as an advocate.[3]

Few have been more adept or more inveterate advocates than William Butler Yeats. Even with the secure status of old age, he designed his edition of *The Oxford Book of Modern Verse* to enshrine the nineties poets as the first moderns. "I have tried to include in this book all good poets who have lived or died from three years before the death of Tennyson to the present moment," he declared in the first sentence of his Introduction.[4] The symbolic chronology both slyly proscribes Ten-nyson from the ranks of the moderns and, because he died in 1892, dates the modern period from the onset of the nineties. More subtly, 1889 marks not only the death of the other major Victorian poet, Browning, but also the publication of *The Wanderings of Oisin and Other Poems*, the first book of verse by Yeats himself.

In a much-quoted passage from that Introduction, Yeats recalled of the nineties that "The revolt against Victorianism meant to the young poet a revolt against irrelevant descriptions of nature, the scientific and moral discursiveness of *In Memoriam* . . . the political eloquence of Swinburne, the psychological curiosity of Browning, and the poetical diction of everybody" (Oxf ix). It is a testimony to the power of Yeats's rhetoric that readers often take the passage at face value, not only as an accurate indictment of Victorian poetry but also as though the verse of early Yeats and his aesthetic friends never indulged in irrelevant description, moral (or perhaps amoral) discursiveness, political rhetoric, psychological curiosity, or poetical diction. More important, Yeats himself revised that early position nine sections later in the Introduction, where he observes:

> When my generation denounced scientific humanitarian preoccupation, psychological curiosity, rhetoric, we had not found what ailed Victorian literature. . . . The mischief began at the end of the seventeenth century, when man became passive before a mechanized nature; that lasted to our own day with the exception of a brief period between Smart's *Song to David* and the death of Byron, wherein imprisoned man beat upon the door. Or I may dismiss all that ancient history and say it began when Stendhal described a masterpiece as a 'mirror dawdling down a lane'. (Oxf xxvii)

This second passage indicts the Victorians more deeply for denying those active forces of mind which power imaginative vision and without which poetry lapses into mere mimesis and criticism of life. The indictment thus suggests an evolution in Yeats's response to the Victorians, in which growing concern for mental action replaces earlier exposure of technical flaws. Perhaps most important, the argument culminates Yeats's lifelong habit of seeing Browning and Tennyson as failed Romantics. For the charmed period between Smart and Byron is, of course, the romantic one, which Yeats looked to for the kinds of acts of mind that informed his own best work. The Victorians failed to continue it. The rhetoric of Yeats's criticism characteristically renders writers important to him in terms of their relation to romanticism. Dante, as we have seen, functioned as a perfected Romantic, free of their supposed frailties. Correspondingly, Tennyson and Browning enter Yeats's prose as anti-Dantes, sapped by the faults and forsaken by the strengths of romanticism. In *The Oxford Book* they embody Victorian mental passivity in contrast to romantic action. After praising

the Romantics in the passage just quoted, Yeats immediately con-
tinues:

> There are only two long poems in Victorian literature that
> caught public attention; *The Ring and the Book* where great
> intellect analyses the suffering of one passive soul, . . . and
> *The Idylls of the King* where a poetry in itself an exquisite
> passivity is built about an allegory where a characterless king
> represents the soul.

The parallel critique of Tennyson and Browning in *The Oxford Book*
reflects a more pervasive parallelism in Yeats's overall responses. Al-
though he distinguished Tennyson's early aestheticism and later didac-
ticism from Browning's youthful subjectivity and later psychologizing,
he often pressed the two of them into the same niche of his poetic
pantheon. The dominant figures of the old generation became the
established antagonists against which the new defined itself. Upon the
death of each, Yeats wrote a guardedly appreciative tribute in the early
nineties. And in each case a central text for the relation of Victorian
poetics to romanticism—Browning's essay on Shelley and Hallam's
essay on Tennyson as heir of Keats and Shelley—so captured Yeats's
allegiance that he cited it again and again in his own polemics. He
could do so because their early identification with the Romantics and
later distance matched the arc of his own career from its Blakean and
Shelleyan origins to its Yeatsian culmination. That arc offered different
perspectives on the Victorians at different points. To young Yeats, firm
in his romantic convictions, Browning and Tennyson had deviated
from their own youthful Keatsian or Shelleyan idealism into at best a
Wordsworthian compromise whose impurities had corrupted the course
of nineteenth-century poetry. Yeats was invoking romantic grand-
fathers against the oppressive paternal dominance of the Victorian
generation. Yet his maneuver brought respite rather than resolution,
since sides changed as Yeats grew older. He, too, repudiated the
romanticism of his youth. Yeats then had to steer between the Scylla of
relapse into an outworn creed, which would perpetuate him as a
diminutive Shelley, and the Charybdis of imitating the form of reac-
tion of his immediate forerunners, which would have changed him only
into a miniature Browning or Tennyson. The literal incorporation of

Browning's verse into Yeats's own poetry—in a late poem with the significant title "Are You Content?"—signals a confidence that can separate itself from both place of origin and pattern of reaction even while declaring its vital mode of continuance. To appreciate that declaration we need to examine Yeats's engagement with Tennyson and Browning more closely.

Attribution of anti-Victorian animus to Yeats (and to many other moderns) errs by replacing a complex reaction with only one of its parts. Admittedly, in describing his generation's quarrel with Browning and Tennyson in *The Oxford Book*, Yeats did for once remember accurately and resist mythology. Over half a dozen pronouncements during the nineties and several later recollections display a consistency of attack. For example, "The Autumn of the Body" (1898) repeats phrases from the review of "Mr. Symons' New Book" (1897) in arguing that

> The poetry which found its expression in the poems of writers like Browning and Tennyson . . . pushed its limits as far as possible, and tried to absorb into itself the science and politics, the philosophy and morality of its time; but a new poetry, which is always contracting its limits, has grown up under the shadow of the old.[5]

Conflating that passage with the other anathemas and credos which Yeats so fondly compiled suggests the foil against which he clarified his own vision. Against an "impure" poetry which strove didactically to interpret the world and to offer a criticism of life to a large public, he urged a "pure" poetry which sought lyrically to revive dreams and passion by considering the world a dictionary of types and symbols and to offer personal intensity to a select few. Ultimately, science would yield to a new religious spirit, however idiosyncratically defined. This use of Tennyson and Browning as poetic Pharisees is familiar to literary history, but it is only part of the story.

To begin with, for Yeats there were at least two Tennysons. Unlike the official and officious poet laureate of middle and old age, the young Tennyson incarnated the very principles Yeats adopted. That Tennyson had inspired the most formative manifesto to Yeats's own development. "When I began to write I avowed for my principles those of Arthur Hallam in his essay upon Tennyson," he declared in "Art and

Ideas" (E&I 347). Yeats summarized those principles repeatedly, perhaps most fully in his review of Lionel Johnson's *Ireland, with Other Poems*:

> Arthur Hallam distinguishes in the opening of his essay on Tennyson between what he calls 'the aesthetic school of poetry,' founded by Keats and Shelley, and the various popular schools. 'The aesthetic school' is, he says, the work of men whose 'fine organs' have 'trembled with emotion, at colours and sounds and movements unperceived by duller temperaments,' 'a poetry of sensation rather than of reflection,' 'a sort of magic producing a number of impressions too multiplied, too minute, and too diversified to allow of our tracing them to their causes, because just such was the effect, even so boundless and so bewildering, produced on their imaginations by the real appearance of nature.' Because this school demands the most close attention from readers whose organs are less fine, it will always, he says, be unpopular compared to the schools that 'mix up' with poetry all manner of anecdotes and opinions and moral maxims. This little known and profound essay defines more perfectly than any other criticism in English the issues in that war of schools which is troubling all the arts. . . .[6]

Hallam's principles of aesthetic purity—the primacy of sensation over reflection and the necessary unpopularity of a poetry free from didacticism and opinion—clearly match the terms in which young Yeats defended his own endeavor, as we have already seen. Only in the essay entitled "On Some of the Characteristics of Modern Poetry, and on the Lyrical Poems of Alfred Tennyson" Hallam had claimed Tennyson as embodiment rather than enemy of his school. But then, Hallam intended his 1831 essay to defend Tennyson's *Poems, Chiefly Lyrical* (1830) and had died three years later, before his friend had changed essentially as poet. The author of "Recollections of the Arabian Nights" or "The Ballad of Oriana" rather than of *In Memoriam* or *Idylls of the King* had prompted Hallam's praise. Tennyson had at that time written only what Yeats, in still another exposition of the essay, termed "his earlier and greater, but less popular, poems" (UP2 130).

This bifurcation of Tennyson enabled Yeats to transfer Hallam's rhetorical strategy to his own campaigns. Just as Hallam had cast the young Tennyson as continuer of the purified romantic tradition bequeathed by Keats and Shelley, so did Yeats champion a return to Shelleyan subjectivity against Tennyson's own later work. There Tennyson had lapsed into the very Wordsworthian moralism to which Hallam objected and which Yeats thought had infected nineteenth-century poetry with an Arnoldian itch to criticize life. Unlike Keats and Shelley—or Blake—argued Yeats, "Tennyson or Wordsworth . . . have troubled the energy and simplicity of their imaginative passions by asking whether they were for the helping or for the hindrance of the world" (E&I 113). Didacticism could contaminate technique as well;[7] Yeats ascribed the weakness of Aubrey De Vere's rendering of Irish tales to "a Tennysonian-Wordsworthian elaboration which lets most of the old wine flow out" (UP1 381). Young Yeats thus dramatized himself as heir to a romantic aesthetic tradition exemplified by Keats, Shelley, Hallam, and early Tennyson against the heresies of Wordsworth, Arnold, and later Tennyson.

A request from *The Bookman* to review Tennyson's last volume, *The Death of Oenone*, after his death in 1892 drove Yeats beyond the resources of mere bifurcation. If he could not wholeheartedly praise the recently deceased laureate, neither could he attack him with propriety. As Matthew Arnold had observed in his introduction to *The Study of Celtic Literature*, "When an acquaintance asks you to write his father's epitaph, you do not generally seize that opportunity for saying that his father was blind of one eye, and had an unfortunate habit of not paying his tradesmen's bills."[8] Instead, Yeats produced a tribute which, sugared with some routine compliments, combined thoughtful appreciation with decorous dissent in ways that would later qualify his early antagonism. He began by noting the common predicament of all modern writers in "being born in a lyrical age" inimical to epic achievement.[9] Continually lured from lyric intensity to ill-fated ventures into vaster forms, Tennyson succeeded best in the *Idylls* until his late return to lyric in the *Tiresias* volume and the final *Death of Oenone*. In those he shed his "hopes based upon mere mechanical change and mere scientific or political inventiveness, until at the last his soul came near to standing, as the soul of the poet should, naked under the heavens." Though too impressed by the reality of the external world, he was "scarce less of a visionary in some ways than Blake himself." Yeats commended the "vivid personal exaltation" of poems like "Akbar's

Dream" and "Telemachus" even while conceding that had Tennyson remained more Shelleyan he would not have supplemented his subjective work with "the miraculous observation and penetrating satire of 'The Churchwarden and the Curate.' "[10] He passed over such performances as "Riflemen, Form" in tactful silence.

The review goes as far as Yeats could toward rehabilitating Tennyson by making Tennyson's reaction against his own and Hallam's subjectivity into a lengthy middle phase redeemed by partial return at the end. It thus prefigures the pattern Yeats later detected in his own career. As that career developed, he began to see Tennyson's fall as in some ways fortunate. If impurities like natural description, moralism, and brooding over scientific opinion "so often extinguished the central flame in Tennyson" (E&I 163), they also preserved him from too cloistered a virtue. By 1926 Yeats could admit after still another summary of Hallam, "I now see that the literary element in painting, the moral element in poetry, are the means whereby the two arts are accepted into the social order and become a part of life and not things of the study and the exhibition" (Au 490).[11] The trick was to incorporate reflection without allowing it to extinguish sensation.

Dropping his worry over Tennysonian impurities, Yeats became obsessed instead with the psychology that had created *In Memoriam*. For the forty years from 1896 onwards, he repeatedly cited Verlaine's aphorism that "Tennyson is too noble, too *anglais;* when he should have been broken-hearted, he had many reminiscences."[12] It is common to dismiss this quip to the company of gibes like Lady Gregory's that "Tennyson had the British Empire for God, and Queen Victoria for Virgin Mary."[13] Yet even Lady Gregory owned signed likenesses of Tennyson and Browning which Yeats could have seen every time he passed through the hall at Coole (Au 391). Verlaine's remark haunted him rather because it epitomized the peril of his own poetic endeavor. Yeats, too, developed a poetry of memory and loss, in which he sought to inject a Blakean and Shelleyan visionary power into a mode which Wordsworth and Tennyson had claimed as their own. How many of his great mature lyrics depend upon the recuperation of memory? The danger was that he, too, might lose intensity, might degenerate from passion into mere recollection. For the poet of the Maud poems, of "Among School Children" or "The Circus Animals' Desertion" among other works, Verlaine's protest tolled a continual tocsin.

If Tennyson evolved into a warning, Browning developed into a danger. Yeats admired him more from the start,[14] cited him more frequently in his published works (some fifty times, compared to about forty for Tennyson), and composed a memorial essay upon his death, just as he later reviewed Tennyson's posthumous volume. But much more important, the critical work that governed Yeats's response and rivalled even Hallam's essay on Tennyson in impact was Browning's own essay on Shelley. As Yeats well knew, he and Browning shared the same forerunner in Shelley and saw him in similar ways. The essay's schema of subjective and objective poetry threatened to decree a common form of reaction as well. In that case the masks that helped Yeats to escape from Shelleyan imitation would carry him only as far as modernizing Browning. He took particular care to denounce Browning's "psychological curiosity" and to articulate the very different psychology underlying his own art. He spoke little of the monologues and concentrated on the safer *The Ring and the Book*, which he at least preferred to *Idylls of the King*. And finally, he felt secure enough to incorporate his favorite Browning passage—the image of the old hunter from *Pauline*—into his own work.

For his memorial notice "Browning" in the Boston *Pilot* (1890), Yeats sounded three themes which even then implicitly paralleled his own situation and which continued to attract him later. One was biographical. Like Yeats himself, Browning emerged as "a mystic."[15] Indeed, Yeats seemed incapable of admiring any poet not a mystic, and with varying degrees of accuracy he also attached that label to Dante, Blake, Shelley, and Tennyson. Later, Yeats would note other biographical parallels, such as Browning's commerical success on the American stage or his long struggle for public acceptance.[16] Second, Yeats rightly forbade the imputation of facile optimism to Browning and provocatively saw that "thought and speculation were to Browning means of dramatic expression much more than aims in themselves." That same feature would pervade Yeats's own mature work, from the dialectics of "Ego Dominus Tuus" through those of "Lapis Lazuli" and "Under Ben Bulben." The key word was "dramatic," and Yeats thought that Browning had sometimes dramatized himself, as in "the great reverie of the Pope in *The Ring and the Book*," just as the future owner of Thoor Ballylee would sometimes do. Finally, Browning had "the most absorbing interest" in life of any modern. He perceived the world as a great boardinghouse full of bustle. Positively, that hurly-burly could impart vitality and "joy itself," but negatively it could destroy unity:

"Sometimes the noise and restlessness got too much into his poetry, and the expression became confused and the verse splintered and broken." The charge of fragmentation seems less illuminating as a judgment on Browning's verse than as an expression of Yeats's early fear that worldly immersion would disrupt the surface of his own idealized poetry, with its theme of Intellectual Beauty. That theme he, like Browning, identified with Shelley.

Support for a poetry of Intellectual vision lay in Browning's "Essay on Shelley," which, together with Shelley's own *Defence of Poetry* and Hallam's essay, Yeats judged the most "philosophic . . . fundamental and radical" work of modern criticism (UP1 277). Suppressed in 1852 when the collection of letters it was meant to introduce turned out to be forgeries, that essay first appeared in 1888 and seemed a contemporary call to the young Yeats. He heeded it selectively. Browning had distinguished the subjective from the objective poet as one who chooses Platonic ideas rather than external things as subjects, adopts the role of seer rather than fashioner as poet, and appeals to the One rather than to the common understanding of men. Exemplifying the objective poet in Shakespeare and the subjective one in Shelley, Browning praised both kinds and proposed a fusion as best of all. The essay hinted at Browning's own progress from a Shelleyan toward a more objective poetry and culminated with revising Shelley into an embryonic Christian. In contrast, Yeats ignored both the objective and objectionable components to respond exclusively to the subjective one as a program for his own poetry. He particularly liked to cite Browning's synopsis of subjective subject matter—"the *Ideas* of Plato, seeds of creation lying burningly on the Divine Hand."[17] This amounts to escaping the mature Browning by returning to the original enthusiasm with which he had pursued the same youthful model as Yeats. The true poetic line thus ran from Shelley through early Browning to Yeats himself. This lineage became harder to defend as Yeats matured.

At first he could lump Browning with other Victorians as lapsed questers. The retrospective *Oxford Book* Introduction accurately reflected his position in the nineties. To Yeats then, Browning should have remained the subjective poet of his own essay. Instead, Browning had fallen into an interpretive mode which derived from Wordsworthian rather than Blakean, Shelleyan, or Keatsian romanticism and led inevitably to Arnoldian canons of criticism. Properly understood, Yeats's celebrated sentence in "The Autumn of the Body" laments the triumph of the wrong nineteenth-century tradition: "it was only with the modern poets, with Goethe and Wordsworth and Browning, that poetry gave up the right to consider all things in the world as a dictionary of types and symbols and began to call itself a critic of life and an interpreter of things as they are."[18] The linkage of Browning— as earlier of Tennyson—with Wordsworth rather than with Shelley signals a fall into the "impurities" which corrupted Victorian verse. Browning's psychological subtlety served more to explore actual life than to reveal the hidden life so central to a subjective poet.

Yeats detected the same corruption of a subjective core in *The Ring and the Book*, which he often paired with *Idylls of the King*. Part of the trouble came from the historical situation. Particularly in his youth, Yeats viewed the nineteenth century as a third, essentially lyrical phase succeeding the earlier stages of narrative (both ballad and epic) and dramatic poetry. He resolved the awkward problem of applying that schema to Browning by declaring in one exposition of it that "The form of Browning is more commonly than not dramatic or epic, but the substance is lyrical" (UP1 271). In aspiring to larger forms, then, Tennyson and Browning contradicted the lyrical obligation of their times. Additionally, the unfortunate split in lyric poetry itself damaged their architectonic capacity. "An absorption in fragmentary sensuous beauty" (from Keats and Shelley) or "detachable ideas" (from Words-worth) had led to a failure "in architectural unity, in symbolic impor-tance" (E&I 353–54).[19] Hence, "*The Revolt of Islam, The Excursion, Gebir, Idylls of the King,* even perhaps *The Ring and the Book,* which fills me with so much admiring astonishment that my judgment sleeps, are remembered for some occasional passage, some moment which gains little from the context." Unevenness in individual conception inten-sified the flaw in overall construction. Yeats responded particularly to character. He thought the *Idylls* the best of Tennyson's long works but seldom praised it. Instead, he labelled its women mere "Girton girls" appealing to the English upper-middle class; thought that Arthur and his court could have been great imaginative types but were instead "nothing"; and maintained that the dedication to Albert and Victoria had "cast round the greatest romantic poem of the century a ring of absurdity."[20] In contrast, Browning had created more believable wom-en with a life of their own. Yet an urge not to create "great passions" but rather to criticize life sapped even *The Ring and the Book,* making Pompilia and Guido "but little" (E&I 196–97). Only Browning's Pope continued to evoke admiration. In 1890 Yeats commended "the great reverie of the Pope"; in 1895 he placed the Pope's meditations "among the wisest of the Christian age"; and as late as 1931 he ranked the Pope as perhaps less "romantic" than Shelley's Prometheus but still worthy of the company of traditional figures like the peddler of The Excursion, one of the few Wordsworthian creations he admired.[21]

His partiality toward Browning's Pope reveals one reason why the mature Yeats identified Browning himself as "to me a dangerous influence" (L 759).[22] The danger derived from the psychology driving both poets' masks. In A Vision Yeats describes the True Mask of phase seventeen, to which he assigned himself along with Shelley and Dante, as Simplification through Intensity and the False Mask as Dispersal. Transposed into those terms, Yeats's critiques of Browning arraign him for too often donning false masks that dissipate his creative force rather than true ones that concentrate it into single images of intensity. In the continual charges of "psychological curiosity," curiosity—with its implication of restless dispersal—weighs as heavily as psychological. Porphyria's Lover, the Duke, Andrea, and Lippo represent fragments of a dispersed personality rather than icons of an integrated one. In contrast, Yeats intended his mature masks of wild old wicked man, towered student, or passionate sage to display simplification through intensity. Again, the charge against Browning tells us more of the dangers Yeats feared in his own endeavor and perhaps projected onto his Victorian forerunner than it does of Browning's actual progress. Yeats sought to avoid those entrapments by designing mythic rather than historic masks representing types rather than individuals.[23] Hence, he admired the Pope, perhaps the most traditional of the figures in The Ring and the Book.[24] That persona both revealed and resulted from the acts of mind which Yeats praised in The Oxford Book and which he missed elsewhere in the poem.

Yeats found his favorite mask in all Browning in the image of the old hunter from Pauline. He cited it nearly as often as he did Verlaine's deprecation of Tennyson's In Memoriam. But whereas Tennyson's poem showed the diffuseness of mere recollection, Browning's image displayed the concentration of true reverie. Yeats mentioned it first in discussing Finn and Oisin during his introduction to Lady Gregory's Gods and Fighting Men (1904). Arguing that the Fianna "are hardly so much individual men as portions of universal nature," Yeats asked, "Do we not always fancy hunters to be something like this, and is not that why we think them poetical when we meet them of a sudden, as in these lines in *Pauline:*

> An old hunter
> Talking with gods; or a high-crested chief
> Sailing with troops of friends to Tenedos?"[25]

Browning's image offered the same universality of imaginative type that so attracted Yeats to central characters in Irish mythology. Yeats used it also to describe those historical Irishmen whom he continually sought to mythologize. In 1931, for example, he validated his conception of Berkeley as "an angry, unscrupulous solitary" rather than as "that gregarious episcopal mask" by adducing the lines from *Pauline* as one of his two "favourite quotations" (the other was the Delphic oracle's commemoration of Plotinus [E&I 408–9]).

A *Vision* propounds the psychological principles underlying Yeats's fascination with Browning's hunter. There the image, together with a passage on an ancient king from *Pippa Passes,* illustrates the Mask from phase four. Yeats explains, "The men of the opposite phase, or of the phases nearly opposite, worn out by a wisdom held with labour and uncertainty, see persons of this phase as images of peace" (AV[B] 110). Yeats terms the man of the exactly opposite phase eighteen The Emotional Man and identifies his True Mask as Intensity through Emotion and his False one as Curiosity, the quality for which he insistently impeached Browning. Instead of creating true masks like the aged hunter, the author of *Pauline* too often created false ones through curiosity. His temptation parallels that of the Daimonic Man of the "nearly opposite" phase seventeen, who finds his True Mask in Simplification through Intensity and his False one in Dispersal. Just as Yeats privately placed himself with the official examples of Dante, Shelley, and Landor for phase seventeen, so may we suspect that he privately consigned Browning either to the same phase as himself or else to the company of Goethe and Matthew Arnold in the adjacent phase eighteen, which so closely resembled it.

The broader context of *Pauline* helps explain how a casual image in Browning became so crucial to Yeats. That poem, Browning's first major one, takes its author's relation to Shelley as a chief subject, both explicitly in the long Sun-Treader passages and implicitly through the kind of utterance it contains. Further, the speaker passionately praises

Shelley even while conceding his own distance from his beloved model. The dark italics of such a poem delineated Yeats's own dilemma. And finally, Browning uses the hunter to exemplify his own early identification with the intense images culled from his youthful reading:

> They came to me in my first dawn of life,
> Which passed alone with wisest ancient books,
> All halo-girt with fancies of my own,
> And I myself went with the tale—a god,
> Wandering after beauty—or a giant,
> Standing vast in the sunset—an old hunter,
> Talking with gods—or a high-crested chief,
> Sailing with troops of friends to Tenedos;—
> I tell you, nought has ever been so clear
> As the place, the time, the fashion of those lives.[26]

To Browning those images carried a Homeric intensity, as the reference to Tenedos (where the Greeks went to wait for the Trojans to accept the wooden horse) suggests. That clarity contrasts with the speaker's current confusion. It centers in the participles of single action attached to each figure—*wandering, standing, talking,* and *sailing*. To Yeats, such a passage meshed magically with his own experience, both in its general context of response to Shelley and in its particular details. When young, he, too, had fervently feigned union with romantic literary figures. He recalled in *Reveries over Childhood and Youth,* "I had many idols, and as I climbed along the narrow ledge I was now Manfred on his glacier, and now Prince Athanase with his solitary lamp, but I soon chose Alastor for my chief of men and longed to share his melancholy" (Au 64). In later years he, too, contrasted his confusion with those youthful icons of unity, until he finally made them into masks to manage his own return to Unity of Being. And finally, from Browning's sequence of participial images, Yeats loved the one alluding specifically to language—an old hunter *talking* with the gods. The hunter who moved Browning became the appropriate mask for phase eighteen, just as Shelley's "wandering lovers and sages" who moved Yeats did for phase seventeen.

A lifetime of brooding over Browning culminated in return to the *Pauline* passage in the last stanza of "Are You Content?" (1938). Yeats called attention to that lyric by setting it as conclusion to *New Poems*, the last volume of verse published in his lifetime whose contents he arranged himself. This grand retrospective poem pictures the aged poet calling on his lineal ancestors for two stanzas before invoking literary ones in the third:

> Infirm and aged I might stay
> In some good company,
> I who have always hated work,
> Smiling at the sea,
> Or demonstrate in my own life
> What Robert Browning meant
> By an old hunter talking with Gods;
> But I am not content.   (VP 605)

Just as the speaker in the first two stanzas hopes his verse has not "Spoilt what old loins have sent," so does he here hope not to betray—or to have betrayed—his poetic patrimony. Like Robert Browning, the poet of "Are You Content?" worried a great deal over his relation to Shelley. But he also worried over his relation to Robert Browning. For Yeats, what Browning meant by the hunter (or should have meant) was creation of a mask of simplified intensity which would preserve him from the temptation of dispersal by delivering to him a unified and unifying image of his own imagining. Only thus could Yeats conceive preserving the integrity of poetic youth while providing for the independence of poetic maturity. The allusion to *Pauline* carries the full network reticulated in the prose about both that passage and its author. It also adds two new perspectives. First, the speaker assigns embodiment of the hunter image to his life rather than his work. The intellect of man—or at least of Yeats—was forced to choose, and in rejecting perfection of the life Yeats here opts instead for continued pursuit of perfection in the work. Even more important, Yeats beats Browning at his own game of masking. For he co-opts Browning into his own poem as an alternate mask. In rejecting that mask, he both distances himself from a dangerously attractive model and yet incorporates that model into his own work. The act establishes himself and Browning as true yet separate brothers of a company that sang after Shelley and the other Romantics. In "Are You Content?" Yeats himself becomes in his work, though not life, an old hunter talking with his poetic gods.[27]

Conceiving such conversations as a series of postromantic encounters establishes a broad paradigm for literary history. It is capacious enough to subsume many components. For example, formally it can include the rise of the dramatic monologue, the revision of the Greater Romantic Lyric, or the struggle to compose a postromantic epic. Thematically, it can embrace the dramatization of Idealist, folk, or national materials; romanticism itself may be the ultimate paradigm of subsequent lost causes. The displacement of religious imagery onto secular experience or the continual tension between the public, prophetic stance and the private concern for lyrical moments belong to the same phenomenon. The concept of a postromantic progression both catches such diverse materials and composes them into a significant pattern. For fundamentally, every major poet of the past century and a half has defined himself in relation to such a tradition, whether viewed positively or negatively. That principle holds not only for Browning, Tennyson, or Yeats, but for poets less often contemplated in this way, like Eliot, Stevens, or Pound. Moreover, the self-definition follows the same pattern—early identification with romanticism or postromanticism, then reaction against that regency, and finally partial restoration.

The Victorians, for example, commonly created a private or confessional poetry of personal longing before projecting themselves into more public or social expression. The early Tennyson strove for a poetry of exquisite sensation deeply derived from romantic examples; after the "decade of silence," however, his verse began to incorporate the very "reflection" which Hallam had praised him for refining away. Similarly, Browning's career approximates the progression of his essay on Shelley from subjective, frankly confessional composition toward a more "objective" stance stemming particularly from his use of masks (though Browning never became so wholly objective as he liked to maintain). With Yeats, both the last great nineteenth-century poet and the first great modern one, the dialectics become more complicated. On the one hand, he began with adaptation of Blakean or Shelleyan norms, progressed through a phase of movement downwards upon life in which his temporary antiromanticism fits his own early work better than it does high romanticism itself, and finally secured enough confidence in his self-definition to label himself a "last romantic" without fear of being a mere follower. On the other hand, Browning and Tennyson first figured as betrayers of an ideal youthful romanticism and then threatened to dominate the form of Yeats's own reaction against that romanticism; they became alternate rivals to self-definition with whom, too, he partially reconciled himself at the end. The double dialectic continues in the most vociferously antiromantic moderns, Pound and Eliot, both of whom produced juvenilia full of attenuated filaments of a debased romantic tradition. In maturity Eliot most often pummeled the Romantics as projections of his deepest fears about his own imagination before modulating into the harmonies of *Four Quartets* and the moderation of his later criticism, and the importance of Tennyson to him has become increasingly clear. Pound continued perhaps the most militant of all, even while producing in *The Pisan Cantos* the most notable epic of imagination and memory since *The Prelude;* his central and acknowledged relation to Browning, examined in the next chapter, still remains to be located in a more generalized postromantic context. Stevens, like Yeats, remained more overt in his relation to his forerunners, and in the 1930s defined his own mature strategy as quest for a "new romanticism."[28]

All this need not make us, or our view of these poets, as "anxious" as some recent criticism would have us. For the history of poetry in English for the last two centuries has not reflected a poetic decline toward a Beckett-like endgame, but rather a series of co-equal achievements. The special puzzle is the hold of those Romantics who died young over those successors who did not. The early deaths of the second romantic generation transfigured them into perpetual icons of poetic youth and integrity, providing the models to which subsequent writers attached themselves. Success in resolving allegiance to an early ideal of the poetic character with the stress of aging and independence may be the central determinant of the success or failure in the later careers of the much longer-lived successors. And each subsequent generation of successors had to cope with previous resolutions as well. The most fortunate of them could say, as Pound did to that American contemporary of the Victorians, Walt Whitman:

> I have detested you long enough.
> I come to you as a grown child
> Who has had a pig-headed father;
> I am old enough now to make friends.
>
> . . . .
> We have one sap and one root—
> Let there be commerce between us.[29]

9 Pound's Parleyings with Browning

In the summer of 1907 a young graduate student at the University of Pennsylvania recorded in a journal a conversation at once traumatic and comic with Professor Felix Schelling over his future. Schelling had told him that because of his writing "I 'was wasting both my own time and that of my instructors by continuing longer at any institution of learning.' He didn't intend it as a compliment. 'You are either a genius or somewhat of a humbug. When you prove that you are a genius I will apologize.'" In the same unpublished journal the young student recorded his devotion not to academia as represented by Schelling but to poetry as represented by Browning. "As grass blade in its sheathe, so are we like in tendency, thou Robert Browning and myself. And so I take no shame to grow from thee."[1] The student was the iconoclastic Ezra Pound, and over the next two decades he would prove that he was more genius than humbug and would exchange friendly letters with his former professor. He would also make clear his devotion to Robert Browning, both in published work and in letters to others. For example, he used two foreign languages to tell the French critic René Taupin in 1928 that "überhaupt ich stamm aus Browning. Pourquoi nier son père?" (Generally, I derive from Browning. Why deny one's father?).[2]

Pound avowed the importance of Browning to him over his entire career, especially during the crucial decade or so stretching from composition of the *A Lume Spento* poems (published 1908) to the appearance of *Three Cantos* in 1917. Other poets, of course, affected Pound deeply—Homer, Ovid, and Dante among them—but Browning held a special place as Pound's immediate major English predecessor. Each was the leading figure of his generation to develop a postromantic substitution of history—particularly the written documents of both social and cultural achievement—for nature as prime stimulus to the poet's internal powers. Each interacts with past figures both by the direct creation of quasi-historical masks (like Browning's Pictor Ignotus or Pound's Bertrans de Born) and by a more complex process of creating a persona which then struggles to re-create a predecessor (as in Browning's *Balaustion's Adventure* and *Sordello* or Pound's "Near Perigord" and *Three Cantos*).[3] Tracing Pound's complex parleyings with Browning requires three departures from contemporary models of influence study. First, I shall make extensive use of unpublished manuscript materials which display the dynamics of influence more clearly than do the final products in the collected works. Second, in contrast to the disappearance of the author in current theories of intertextuality, Pound insists not only that his texts answer to Browning's but that he himself speaks directly to Browning himself (as when he titles a poem "To R.B.," addresses "Master Bob Browning," or exclaims in vexation, "Hang it all, Robert Browning"). And third, by way of conclusion I shall suggest why the anxiety model of literary influence applies less well to poets like Pound than to those more directly in the romantic tradition.

I begin not with the customary starting point of *A Lume Spento* but with Pound's unpublished prose speculations on Browning and the related poem "To R.B.," itself only recently published in a problematic transcription. The prose speculations occupy eight pages of a typescript made with a blue ribbon and currently in a folder at the Pound Archive of the Beinecke Library. The account seems to alternate between being a diary and a letter, with occasional verse patched in; for lack of a better term, I refer to it as a journal and have already quoted its account of the conversation with Schelling and oath of allegiance to Browning. In meditating on literature and on young Pound's own literary predicament, the remainder of the eight pages utilize Browning in three major ways: to indicate the kind of misapprehension of Browning against which Pound reacted, to focus a theory of literary influence on Browning, and to identify the unexpected source of Browning's early impact on Pound through the long poems *Balaustion's Adventure* and *Aristophanes' Apology*.

Throughout his career Pound loved to contrast his own enthusiasms with the denseness of a more orthodox voice, and in the early journal Edmund Clarence Stedman plays a role that would later feature Lascelles Abercrombie, Palgrave's *Golden Treasury*, or the hapless Hermann Hagedorn. Pound writes:

> When Stedman talks of some of Browning as "impertinent verses" and again of "poetry that neither gods nor man can understand," he out of his banking house presumes to judge all other divine and human intellect by his own—for which presuming I question, to say the least, his tact. Even tho these phrases be slung in with some [of] what is intended as praise of Browning's poetry, we must quietly remember that it is only Mr. Stedman trying to squeeze infinity into an oyster shell, To bound creation by the borough of Bronx.
>
> E.C.S. is here objecting to the "prose run mad" stanzas ending
>
> > Who fished the murex up
> > What porridge had John Keats.
>
> I hope he begins to comprehend it by this time although I feel pretty sure that it was not (it the porridge was not) the Battle Creek health food that much contemporary verse seems to be written on.

Although Pound does not say so, he is reacting to Stedman's influential study *Victorian Poets*, first published in 1875, which went through thirteen editions by 1887 and was revised in 1893.[4] Stedman there saw Tennyson as showing "every aspect of poetry as an art, and the best average representation of the modern time," while he took a more mixed view of Landor and Browning. Pound customarily reversed this distinction, seeing Browning as the greatest poet of his age and Landor as the most complete man of Victorian letters. More important, he would later insist on Browning's clarity and would interpret hostile charges of incomprehension as indicating only the critic's failure to grasp Browning's aims.

   In contrast to Stedman's criticism and verse, Pound set up as a wholehearted admirer of Browning in prose and hoped to imitate him in poetry. On the page after berating Stedman, Pound wrote:

If one is continuously filled with burnings of admiration for the great past masters so that he runs from sweet flame to sweeter flame and then above it all finds his own proper rapture from within, surely his telling this must have on it the tang and taint of theirs who

> Enter in and take their place there sure enough
> Though they come back and can not tell the world

(for today all roads find Browning.) I think I am beginning to appreciate him with some germ of intelligence.

The lines cited come from Browning's "Andrea del Sarto," where they apply to Raphael and others whose reach exceeds their grasp. But Pound here is not so much a self-critical Andrea as an acolyte who hopes to follow his beloved masters from afar. The "germ of intelligence" in his appreciation would help engender a whole career.

Pound began the journal by declaring his allegiance to past poets, particularly Dante and Browning, in a combination of bravado and almost embarrassing adoration. Their great discoveries meant that a later poet had either to follow them or else to condemn himself to minor status:

> Are our riming and our essays to be confined only to such secondary things as missed the eyes of our fore-goers? Dante, Browning, and a half hundred others are not known in detail to a dozen men, and when one stumbles of a flaming blade that pierces him to extacy is he to hide it for some rabbit fear of "copyist" "blind follower" or alley taunt "He hath not thought's originality"? Is it, tell me whether, is it more original to cry some great truth higher and more keen, to add a candle to the daylight that none see, or to reverse some million proverbs that the mob may laugh to see the worthies butt-end up displayed to common view?

That exclamation captures several hallmarks of Pound's later thought—the numbering of Dante and Browning among his major influences, the sense of a small minority of cultured men continuing and advancing civilization, the notion of ecstasy as the ideal response to great art, and scorn for those who disagree. At this stage identification with the earlier poets is nearly total, and Pound will shortly find ways to strive for his own independence. But in so doing he will follow the model not of an anxious agon with his predecessors but rather of a masked dialogue with them; the early identification here will yield to a sense of fellow-craftsmanship in a literary history governed by an ideogrammic rather than a linear conception.

The focus of speculation on literary influence in the journal swiftly narrows to just Browning, and in particular to his long, late, and now-neglected poems *Balaustion's Adventure* and *Aristophanes' Apology*, both of which use the persona of the Greek maid Balaustion as a mask for Browning to work out his own relationship to his admired Euripides. Pound follows the simile of his resemblance to Browning being like that of a grass blade to its sheathe with the admission that he himself may be "less near may hap to life and rooted things, less 'human with' my 'droppings of warm tears.'" The allusion is to the description of Euripides in line 2412 and again in 2671 of *Balaustion's Adventure* and already exemplifies Pound's early skill in the art of making it new. For Browning not only has Balaustion apply the title "The Human with his droppings of warm tears"[5] to Euripides but also borrows that line from his wife Elizabeth's *Wine of Cyprus* and uses it for the motto of his own poem. In citing the phrase, Pound aligns himself with Browning in using a previous poet's words to describe his own relation to an admired forerunner. Similarly, at the bottom of the same page Pound notes Browning's debt to Shakespeare in the passage of the sequel poem *Aristophanes' Apology* ending "Philemon, thou shalt see Euripides / Clearer than mortal sense perceived the man." Paradoxically, masks and literary tradition could lead to seeing a poet plain.

After developing his own thoughts on literary influence in a page of Keatsian doggerel ("And sith our keener beauties sooth may be / The half known strains of older balladry / . . . crouching deep / Within the caverns that old verses keep / I bear the waters of more shadowed springs"), Pound arrives at the formulation most helpful for understanding his intense relation to Browning over the next decade. He writes, "Just my luck, confounded and delightful, that after I had threshed these things out for myself I find 'Balaustion's Adventure' holds them better said, and said some sooner. As my Browning has not lines numbered I can not refer other than to Macmillan edit. p. 661." Turning to page 661 of the two-volume Macmillan edition of *The*

Poetical Works of Robert Browning published in 1902, the year in which
Pound began to study Browning seriously,[6] we find Balaustion refusing
to worry over Sophokles' intention to write a new play on the Alcestis
story just dramatized by Euripides: "no good supplants a good, / Nor
beauty undoes beauty." She continues,

> Still, since one thing may have so many sides,
> I think I see how,—far from Sophokles,—
> You, I, or anyone might mould a new
> Admetos, new Alkestis. Ah, that brave
> Bounty of poets, the one royal race
> That ever was, or will be, in this world!
> They give no gift that bounds itself and ends
> I' the giving and the taking: theirs so breeds
> I' the heart and soul o' the taker, so transmutes
> The man who only was a man before,
> That he grows godlike in his turn, can give—
> He also: share the poets' privilege,
> Bring forth new good, new beauty, from the old.
> As though the cup that gave the wine, gave, too,
> The God's prolific giver of the grape,
> That vine, was wont to find out, fawn around
> His footstep, springing still to bless the dearth,
> At bidding of a Mainad. So with me:
> For I have drunk this poem, quenched my thirst,
> Satisfied heart and soul—yet more remains!
> Could we too make a poem? Try at least,
> Inside the head, what shape the rose-mists take!

Balaustion's speech amounts to a theory of literary influence. She
sees the process not as an anxious contest but as a transmission of
power. Far from intimidating future efforts, the force of a great work
actually engenders them; it "breeds" and "transmutes" the later poet
into a creative divinity of his own to "bring forth new good, new beauty
from the old." Her obscure simile of the grape, appropriate to the
Dionysiac festival at which Greek tragedies were performed, implies a
transmission not simply of the work but of the power that produced the
work in the first place. Having "drunk this poem," she now thinks to
make one: "Could we too make a poem?" The new work does not

threaten the old but rather, since things have many sides, helps make up a part of an ideal order of poetry.

The obvious connection of Balaustion's ideas to Pound not only in 1907 but also throughout his career becomes clearer in context of the work from which they come. Set at the time of the Athenian defeat in the Peloponnesian War, *Balaustion's Adventure* dramatizes the saving of a group of Athenian loyalists from the island of Kameiros. In an adaptation of historical accounts of the Syracusans' willingness to free Athenian captives who could recite passages of Greek tragedy, Browning has Balaustion earn the Kameireans' safety by timely recital of Euripides' tragedy *Alcestis*. Using Balaustion as a mask, Browning presents a narrative account framing a free translation of the entire *Alcestis* and concluding with an original, alternate telling of the story. The poem itself thus enacts the premises of Balaustion's notion of literary influence, in which a later poet both takes power from an earlier one and simultaneously revivifies his work. We have only to think of Pound's *Cantos* to ponder another long poem which depends on masks, both draws power from and actually translates a Greek work, and insists on the social efficacy of literature. Further, like the *Cantos* with their retelling of Homer's Nekyia, *Balaustion's Adventure* chooses for retelling a Greek work involving a hero's descent to Hades. Browning's full impact on the *Cantos* involves *Sordello*, *Balaustion's Adventure*, and the sequel *Aristophanes' Apology* (which this time translates the *Heracles* of Euripides). But in 1907 that work was nearly a decade away. Browning's ability to "transmute" Pound's own powers would first breed a series of shorter monologues.

Among the early monologues, the recently discovered "To R.B." bears the closest relation to *Balaustion's Adventure* and Pound's responses to it. The R.B. of the title is, of course, Robert Browning, but the speaker is not yet the "E.P." by which the author would later mask himself. Rather, he is a minor poet of the 1870s. Because the only published transcription of the poem lacks Pound's introductory note on the speaker, I quote that note here by way of clarification: "In the early 'seventies' one John Cowper of the 'Minores' met Browning and talked with him concerning a new poem containing a transcript from Euripides. As the others, seeing them talking earnestly drew aside, Cowper's talk became more animated."[7] Lest the point be missed, Pound scrawled by hand on the typescript, "See Browning's 'Balaustion's Apology,'" a title which conflates *Balaustion's Adventure* (1871) with

the later *Aristophanes' Apology* (1875). *Balaustion's Adventure* is dedi-
cated to Countess Cowper, and the Cowper of Pound's poem stands in
the same relation to Browning that the Balaustion of Browning's does
to Euripides and, later, Aristophanes. Both function as masks for the
author's wrestling with his relation to an admired forerunner; both
poems take that relation as their true subjects.

Pound's Cowper mask shares suspiciously many traits with Pound
himself. For example, both admire Cavalcanti and hope to use him as
Browning used Sordello, as Cowper makes clear in prose before shifting
to verse. His first metaphor employs the image of breaking wood, which
Pound would later apply to himself and Whitman: "Lo thou one
branch, and I / A smaller stem have broken, / Both of one tree. . . ."
More important, Pound's poem follows the same view of literary influ-
ence upheld in Browning's. After describing Balaustion's devotion to
Euripides in words borrowed from Browning himself ("thy words I
borrow / Being best man's words I know"), Cowper responds to the
charge that Balaustion sings with others' music: "Nay we all sing others
music, / Would we, would we not." Nonetheless, he and Browning
both strive to imitate Balaustion. Following the extended metaphor of
the poet as providing not all truth but simply enough to pay an
innkeeper on a journey, Cowper berates himself for confusion (as more
than one of Pound's later speakers would do) and claims an important
though lesser role than Browning:

> But I ramble as ever,
> Thought half-cut from next thought—
> Two radii ill seen are blurred to one.
>
> . . . .
> Thou swing'st the texts great line
> For the full synagogue, too high
> —we use not millions for the children's sum—
> Thou singst the text. I in my lesser place
> Make plain the meaning to some dozen nearest me.

Like Balaustion, Cowper insists that the relation of successive poets is
cooperative rather than antagonistic: "One fellow broke the path. / I
blaze the trees—So piecemeal make we road." Pound's sophistication
clearly outruns Cowper's, just as Browning's outstrips Balaustion's.
Both Balaustion and Cowper function as simpler masks for their more

complex authors, and for their more complex relation to their forerun-
ners. But while the Browning of *Balaustion* was a great mature poet able
genuinely to revise Euripides even while paying tribute to him, the
Pound of "To R. B." had not yet attained that status, nor would he for
almost a decade. Not until *Three Cantos* would he be able to equal
Browning's dialectics.

In the roughly contemporary "Mesmerism," first published in *A
Lume Spento* and retained in the collected *Personae*, Pound again
addressed Browning directly, this time without a mask. The title
echoes Browning's own poem "Mesmerism," from which Pound also
takes his epigraph:

> Mesmerism
>
> "And a cat's in the water-butt."—Robert Browning
>
> Aye you're a man that! ye old mesmerizer
> Tyin' your meanin' in seventy swadelin's,
> One must of needs be a hang'd early riser
> To catch you at worm turning. Holy Odd's bodykins!
>
> "Cat's i' the water butt!" Thought's in your verse-barrel,
> Tell us this thing rather, then we'll believe you,
> You, Master Bob Browning, spite your apparel
> Jump to your sense and give praise as we'd lief do.
>
> You wheeze as a head-cold long-tonsilled Calliope,
> But God! what a sight you ha' got o' our in'ards,
> Mad as a hatter but surely no Myope,
> Broad as all ocean and leanin' man-kin'ards.
>
> Heart that was big as the bowels of Vesuvius,
> Words that were wing'd as her sparks in eruption,
> Eagled and thundered as Jupiter Pluvius,
> Sound in your wind past all signs o' corruption.
>
> Here's to you, Old Hippety-Hop o' the accents,
> True to the Truth's sake and crafty dissector,
> You grabbed at the gold sure; had no need to pack cents
> Into your versicles.
>   Clear sight's elector![8]

Couched in the form, language, and meters of Browning, the poem identifies those characteristics of Browning's poetry which Pound admired and sought to adapt for his own verses. First came apparent difficulty—"tyin' your meanin' in seventy swadelin's"—which signals not arbitrary obscurity but a complex and compressed mode of presentation which draws the reader into its unravelling. A decade later Pound would associate such qualities with his enthusiasms for Chinese and Provençal poetry: "The first great distinction between Chinese taste and our own is that the Chinese *like* poetry that they have to think about, and even poetry that they have to puzzle over. This latter taste has occasionally broken out in Europe, notably in twelfth-century Provence and thirteenth-century Tuscany."[9] Second, the poem admires Browning's expansion of poetic diction to include "unpoetic" phrases like "cat's in the water-butt," which Pound liked enough to use twice in the poem and again as title for an early story published only recently.[10] So, too, did he admire Browning's profundity ("Thought's in your verse-barrel"), psychological insight ("But God! what a sight you ha' got o' our in'ards"), and breadth ("broad as all ocean"). The playful phrase "Old Hippety-Hop o' the accents" suggests by a pun both Browning's innovative metrics (he could break the pentameter nearly as well as Pound) and his use of foreign languages or accents (as in "Soliloquy of the Spanish Cloister") in a way that prefigures Pound's own usage. And finally, Pound praises Browning as "Clear sight's elector." The final phrase gave him trouble: In one manuscript, he first wrote "Lordly as Hector" (which didn't fit the previous characterization), then cancelled that and tried "Minerva's director" (which associated Browning with the goddess of wisdom), and finally made better sense if not much better poetry by choosing "clear sight's elector" (which rightly identified Browning with the process of perception).[11]

Two things which "Mesmerism" does not say are as interesting as those it does articulate. First, the poem remains silent on its own distortion of Browning. Nowhere, for example, does Pound mention Browning's philosophizing and ratiocination or his troubled allegiance to Christianity. Rather, Pound presents a selective sketch which stresses poetic craft and psychological perception. This selectivity results in as much a portrait of Pound as he would like to become as it is of Browning and provides an early ground for Pound's later departure from his sometime model. Second, the poem does not mention masks or the dramatic monologue. But it does create a mask and constitute a monologue. To see that, we need to appreciate the subject of Browning's own poem entitled "Mesmerism," which presents a mesmerist in the act of conjuring up the spirit and form of an absent woman. Browning's mesmerist stands as paradigm for the poet of personae, both creating a character mask and pondering his relation to his own activity. Pound's poem continues the process, in that the author both calls up Browning and suggests his own relation to him. Pound has carried over the preoccupation with a precursor of Browning's Balaustion poems and his own "To R.B.," but this time with a speaker closer to himself.

Other poems from Pound's early period reflect parts of his dialogue with Browning. While Browning wrote *Fifine at the Fair*, Pound responded with "Fifine Answers," a dramatic monologue in which Pound invents a reply for the carnival dancer to a question in Browning's poem; significantly, Pound's Fifine stresses "the work shop where each mask is wrought."[12] To Browning's "Pictor Ignotus" Pound responds with "Scriptor Ignotus," a particularly Browningesque monologue complete with epigraph specifying place and date ("Ferrara 1715"), which concerns a minor English poet's effort to construct an epic rivaling Dante's (CEP 24). Pound liked Browning's poem well enough to borrow a line from it ("These sell our pictures") for "In Durance," in which a Pound-like persona laments his isolation from all save the masks of beauty that swirl around his soul (P 20). Pound's "Paracelsus in Excelsis" forms a mystical consummation of Browning's *Paracelsus*, and Pound's sonnet "To E.B.B." (Elizabeth Barrett Browning) complements the longer "To R.B." Pound also experimented with Browning's adaption of dramatic monologue to the verse epistle. His "Capilupus Sends Greeting to Grotus (Mantua 1500)," for example, echoes the techniques of Browning's "Cleon," "Karshish," and "A Death in the Desert." Less innovative than "Mesmerism" or "To R.B.," these early poems stay closer to imitation than to the originality to which Pound would shortly bring the form.

Taking over the dramatic monologue for his own work, Pound happily acknowledged its immediate source for him in Browning and ultimate origin in classical verse, particularly Ovid. Two weeks before sending her "To R.B.," he wrote to Viola Baxter:

> What part of Browning do or don't you like? People usually begin at [the] wrong end. Try the "Men and Women" in which Cleon, Karshish (The Epistle of), One Word More,

Pictor Ignotus—there are several very nice ones. Ovid be-
gan that particular sort of subjective personality analysis in
his "Heroides" & Browning is after 2000 years about the first
person to do anything more with it. I follow—humbly of
course? doing by far the best job of any of them? not quite.[13]

The poems Pound recommends constitute a special subset within
Browning's dramatic monologues, for they all highlight the speaker's
relation to his discourse as much as the discourse itself. With Cleon and
Karshish the epistle form and special historical relation to Christianity
create such interest, with "One Word More" a poet identified as
"R.B." discusses his relation to his own work, and with "Pictor Ig-
notus" the course of the speaker's utterance reenacts that of his ca-
reer.[14] The list further indicates that Pound has in mind not the
original *Men and Women* volume published in 1855, which includes
poems that are not dramatic monologues and lacks the earlier "Pictor
Ignotus," but rather the *Men and Women* grouping that Browning
devised for the 1863 rearrangement of his poems, where it contains
only dramatic monologues and includes "Pictor." Pound would have
found that arrangement in the 1902 Macmillan edition containing the
passage from *Balaustion's Adventure* cited in the unpublished journal.[15]
He likely had the same grouping in mind a decade later, when he
commended Eliot's achievement in the dramatic monologue: "The
most interesting poems in Victorian English are in Browning's *Men and
Women*, or, if that statement is too absolute, let me contend that the
form of these poems is the most vital form of that period of En-
glish. . . . Since Browning there have been very few good poems of
this sort. Mr. Eliot has made two notable additions to the list" (LE
419–20). Like "The Love Song of J. Alfred Prufrock," some of Pound's
own mature dramatic monologues would constitute "notable addi-
tions" to the genre.

Pound's own definition of his aims parallels Browning's. Stung by the
criticism of the confessional *Pauline* and difficult *Sordello*, Browning
had explained in a note to *Dramatic Lyrics*, his first volume to contain
dramatic monologues: "Such Poems as the majority in this volume
might also come properly enough, I suppose, under the head of 'Dra-
matic Pieces'; being, though often Lyric in expression, always Dramatic
in principle, and so many utterances of so many imaginary persons, not
mine.—R.B." (1:347). In explaining his own aims to William Carlos

Williams in 1908, Pound took over the term which Browning had used as title: "To me the short so-called dramatic lyric—at any rate the sort of thing I do—is the poetic part of a drama the rest of which (to me the prose part) is left to the reader's imagination or implied or set in a short note. I catch the character I happen to be interested in at the moment he interests me, usually a moment of song, self-analysis, or sudden understanding or revelation. . . . I paint my man as I *conceive* him" (L 3–4). The two avowals share emphasis on creation of a character and on drama revealed through discourse; Pound further carries over Browning's stress elsewhere on the cult of the moment. The avowals are also incomplete. For in painting his man as he conceived him, Pound often would make the act of conception his true subject, as in "Near Perigord" or *Three Cantos*; so, too, had Browning, as in *Sordello* or *The Ring and the Book*, which Pound later commended as "serious experimentation" (LE 33). Nor was the separation between poet and persona so distinct from biography as Pound and Browning liked to maintain.

Pound continually emphasized Browning's exile from England to Italy in a way that paralleled his own expatriation from America. "The decline of England began on the day when Landor packed his trunks and departed to Tuscany," he wrote in "How to Read." "Up till then England had been able to contain her best authors; after that we see Shelley, Keats, Byron, Beddoes on the Continent, and still later observe the edifying spectacle of Browning in Italy and Tennyson in Buckingham Palace" (LE 32). Omitting to mention Browning's composition of most of *Sordello* in England before 1840 or his lionization by Victorian London for the last three decades of his life, Pound focused instead on Browning's self-imposed exile, opposition to Victorian literary norms, and long battle against obscurity, in all of which he resembled Pound himself struggling against contemporary America.[16] Pound would later settle in Italy before returning to his native country. But before he did so, he hoped to recover Provençal culture for his own time as Browning had revivified Italian for his. Writing in 1922 to Professor Felix Schelling, who by then had presumably decided that Pound was a genius and not a humbug after all, Pound said of his earlier career: "My assaults on Provence: 1st: using it as a subject matter, trying to do as R.B. had with Renaissance Italy. 2, Diagrammatic translations" (L 179).

Doing for Provence what Browning had done for Italy proceeded by creation of a series of dramatic monologues and masks. These had an intimate relation to the poet's self. As Pound explained in a famous passage from *Gaudier-Brzeska*:

> In the "search for oneself," in the search for "sincere self-expression," one gropes, one finds some seeming verity. One says "I am" this, that, or the other, and with the words scarcely uttered one ceases to be that thing.
>
> I began this search for the real in a book called *Personae*, casting off, as it were, complete masks of the self in each poem. I continued in a long series of translations, which were but more elaborate masks.[17]

These masks comprise a great deal of Pound's work in the decade between *A Lume Spento* and the *Cantos*, including the Troubadour dramatic monologues, the translations in *Cathay* and *Homage to Sextus Propertius*, and the linked series of monologues that comprises the *Mauberley* sequence. Like Browning's, these monologues (except for the Chinese ones) often involve artists or connoisseurs, posit a linkage between artistic and sexual harmony, mix their diction and rhythms, and claim specific historical settings. They also recall Browning explicitly: For example, where Browning's monk begins "Gr-r-r," Pound's Cino begins "Bah!"; Pound thought that "The River-Merchant's Wife: A Letter" might "have been slipped into Browning's work without causing any surprise save by its simplicity and its naive beauty";[18] and the young writer in "Mr. Nixon" invokes Browning's Bishop Blougram. Using masks of poets where Browning more often used those of artists, Pound executes his search for the real by creating a series of personae who externalize various problems in the career of their creator, who also happens to be an innovative but insufficiently appreciated poet. In E.P. and Mauberley, for example, Pound exorcises two threats to his own development—one a projection of what he feared he had been, the other an embodiment of what he feared he might become.[19] Because these monologues form the one aspect of Pound's relationship to Browning that previously has received careful study,[20] I should like to pass on here to Pound's resumption of his direct parleyings with Browning in *Three Cantos*, with its extended response to *Sordello*.

During the decade culminating in *Three Cantos*, Pound's interest in *Sordello* increasingly stressed its dialectics of masking as an exploration of the poet's relation both to his own creations and to his literary predecessors. As early as "To R.B." Pound had his Cowper persona meditate making Cavalcanti into his own analogue for the troubadour Sordello. In the 1913 essay "Troubadours—Their Sorts and Conditions" he naturally coupled Dante and Browning as two poets interested in rendering Sordello in their own work (LE 97). The next year, Pound saw a distinction: "Browning's 'Sordello' is one of the finest *masks* ever presented. Dante's 'Paradiso' is the most wonderful *image*" (GB 86). And the year after that, 1915, he confessed to his father the crucial importance of Browning's work to the *Cantos*, which he was then beginning:

> If you like the "Perigord" you would probably like Browning's "Sordello". . . .
>
> It is a great work and worth the trouble of hacking it out.
>
> I began to get it on about the 6th reading—though individual passages come up all right on the first reading.
>
> It is probably the greatest poem in English. Certainly the best long poem in English since Chaucer.
>
> You'll have to read it sometime as my big long endless poem that I am now struggling with starts out with a barrel full of allusions to "Sordello."[21]

Appearing in *Poetry* magazine for June, July, and August 1917, the first published version of the opening *Three Cantos* did indeed commence with a "barrel full" of allusions to Sordello. These survive in the final form of the poem as the famous apostrophe beginning Canto 2 ("Hang it all, Robert Browning, / there can be but the one 'Sordello'") and the echoing of Browning's description of Venice opening Canto 3 ("I sat on the Dogana's steps / For the gondolas cost too much that year. / And there were not 'those girls,' there was one face"). But where the final poem devotes Canto 1 to the problems and implications of rendering Divus's Homer and alludes only briefly to Browning in Cantos 2 and 3, the original one devoted the first canto to the problems of continuing from Browning, referred to the Victorian writer in Canto 2, and only arrived at Homer in Canto 3. I focus here on the original *Three Cantos* as Pound's last major poetic parleying with Browning.

They opened with a more extended version of the address to Browning, in which the more decorous "Hang it all" replaces the earthier "Damn it all" of the manuscript draft:

Hang it all, there can be but one *Sordello*!
But say I want to, say I take your whole bag of tricks,
Let in your quirks and tweeks, and say the thing's an art-form,
Your *Sordello*, and that the modern world
Needs such a rag-bag to stuff all its thought in:
Say that I dump my catch, shiny and silvery
As fresh sardines flapping and slipping on the marginal cobbles?
(I stand before the booth, the speech; but the truth
Is inside this discourse—this booth is full of the marrow of
    wisdom.)[22]

That passage both identifies *Sordello* as starting point for *Three Cantos*
and salutes Browning in his own language of quirks, tweeks, and
outrageous metaphor. Two points relate particularly to Pound's style of
parleying with Browning. First, he takes over Browning's habit of
portraying his relation to a key precursor. In "To R.B." he had created
a persona in Cowper whose relation to Browning resembled that of
Balaustion to Euripides in *Balaustion's Adventure*. Here, Pound acts
more directly and seizes on a poem where Browning had done likewise.
For just as *Three Cantos* opens with a Pound-like poet meditating on his
relation to Browning, so had *Sordello* begun with a Browning-like figure
working out his relation to his own precursor, Shelley, whom the poem
exorcises implicitly through its historical ground and explicitly as the
early "spirit."[23] Pound's parleying with Browning thus stands in the
tradition of Browning's parleying with Shelley. Further, the celebrated
word "rag-bag" here derives from Browning, who used it in his other
Balaustion poem, *Aristophanes' Apology*, as part of Aristophanes' gibes
at Euripides:

> . . . why trifle time with toys and skits
> When he could stuff four ragbags sausage-wise
> With sophistry, with bookish odds and ends,
> Sokrates, meteors, moonshine, "Life's not Life,"
> "The tongue swore, but unsworn the mind remains,"
> And fifty such concoctions, crab-tree-fruit.   (2:212)

Aristophanes' accusations obviously fit Browning himself—and
Pound—as well as they do Euripides. Yet in taking over the "rag-bag"
charge, Pound subtly shifts the tone from abuse to raillery: His address

to "Robert Browning," as to "Bob Browning" and "Mr. Browning" (117, 118), contains affection and respect as well as exasperation. The opening of *Three Cantos* both states and enacts Pound's continuing insistence on literary influence as a positive process of remaking tradition.

As *Three Cantos* proceeds to appropriate Browning's paratactic presentation of events, use of the narrator as character, and device of the diorama booth,[24] it arrives at a crucial difference. An early draft includes the bold avowal "I'll have up not one man but a crowd of them / Living, & breathing, gouzling & swearing real as Sordello" as well as the more tentative query "You had one whole man? / And I have many fragments, less worth?" retained in *Three Cantos.* These provide the answer to the poem's own question, "What's left for me to do? Whom shall I conjure up; who's my Sordello . . . ?" (115, 117). Creating a host of heroes—Sigismundo, Confucius, Adams, and others—in place of Browning's sole protagonist did help Pound to get beyond Browning's poem. He related them and others partly in a manner which *Three Cantos* 2 describes as "ply over ply," a phrase which survives in the final Cantos 4 and 40, and which Hugh Witemeyer has suggestively explored as a pervasive technique in the *Cantos.* [25] We may add that the phrase itself is Browning's and comes from one of the numerous discussions of poetic art in *Sordello* (5.163).

One trait of Browning's troubled Pound in *Three Cantos*—his looseness with historical fact, which Pound continually excused but just as continually mentioned. Even before starting the poem Pound had noticed but condoned Browning's drastic alteration of Sordello's long and happy life to an early and frustrated death (LE 97). In *Three Cantos* he arraigns and then acquits Browning's great description of the font at Goito so central to the whole of *Sordello:*

> And half your dates are out, you mix your eras;
> For that great font Sordello sat beside—
> 'Tis an immortal passage, but the font?—
> Is some two centuries outside the picture.
> Does it matter?
> Not in the least.   (114)

Yet to Pound it did matter. The *Cantos* involved painstaking research and made insistent claims of accurate referentiality. In elevating the previously vilified Sigismundo to hero, Pound carefully bases his case on actual documents to refute the hostile accounts deriving from Sigismundo's great enemy, Pope Pius II.[26] Whatever the vagaries of the *Cantos* during the middle, Fascist years, the stronger earlier and later ones cling stubbornly to a verifiable scaffold. Pound and Browning both substitute history for nature as stimulus to imagination, but Pound's greater devotion to historical accuracy joined his multiple heroes, his diverse cultures, and his commitment to ideogrammic method in enabling the *Cantos* to take their own shape.

Not surprisingly, Pound's few caustic critiques of Browning cluster around the period when he was revising *Three Cantos* and needed to distance himself from his sometime model. As he explained to Iris Barry in 1916, "The hell is that one catches Browning's manner and mannerisms. At least I've suffered the disease" (L 90). Centering on diction, word order, and a substitution of thought for perception, his various aversions peaked in a 1919 essay objecting to Browning's translation of Aeschylus. There Pound holds that Browning sometimes stooped to "unsayable jargon," failed to realize that inversions suitable to an inflected language violate an uninflected one, and yielded to the seduction of "ideas" (LE 267–68). These criticisms fit the early Pound as well as they do Browning, of course, and did not last long. Pound soon returned to praising Browning's monologues and to associating him with Landor, with musicality, and with serious technical experiment. By the 1930s he recommended reading Browning to Laurence Binyon and to Sarah Perkins Cope, just as he had in 1907 and 1909 to Viola Baxter and William Carlos Williams.[27] And in the *ABC of Reading* he quoted the long passage on the font in *Sordello* against "Victorian half-wits" who missed Browning's limpidity of narration, lucidity of sound, and variety of rhymes (ABCR 188–91).

In the crucial decade culminating in *Three Cantos*, as well as later in his career, Pound's relation to Browning does not follow the anxiety model so pervasive in contemporary notions of literary influence.[28] Though his allegiance wobbled at the time when he needed to cast off *Sordello* from the *Cantos*, the rejection never had that violence or obsessive distortion symptomatic of anxiety. Competitive Pound certainly was, but not anxious in the current sense of that term. Instead, his career exemplified the beneficent conception of literary influence recorded in his student journal and in Browning's Balaustion poems. Three reasons for this present themselves. First, while anxiety theories emphasize the poetic imagination, Pound instead stressed poetic craft. As T. S. Eliot remarked, "Pound's great contribution to the work of other poets is his insistence upon the immensity of the amount of *conscious* labor to be performed by the poet; and his invaluable suggestions for the kind of training the poet should give himself."[29] This concern with technique obviates the anxiety induced by fixation on the act of inspiring or imagining itself; it returns to the notion of the poet as maker. Second, while Pound conceived of literary history as in someways linear in terms of technique, he thought of the products as arranged in an ideogrammic rather than linear or even cyclic order: Major works did not compete with each other but rather built up a field charging each other with energy, as the *Odyssey* did for the *Cantos*. And finally, Pound's firmly comparative stance took him outside his own language to Homer, Ovid, Dante, or Li Po as well as to Whitman, Browning, or Yeats. In contrast, anxiety theories seem to posit a postromantic endgame in English poetry deriving from the blocking figure of Milton. Pound's different conception of poetic art, literary history, and frame of reference enabled him instead to honor and to enlarge the early insights of his graduate days. For him, "the tradition" was always "a beauty which we preserve, and not a set of fetters to bind us" (LE 91).

Notes

CHAPTER 1

1. *The Cantos of Ezra Pound* (New York: New Directions, 1971), pp. 56–57 (Canto XII).

2. For three different but related manifestations of these trends, see Harold Bloom's volumes from *The Anxiety of Influence* (New York: Oxford University Press, 1973) onwards, W. Jackson Bate's *The Burden of the Past and the English Poet* (Cambridge: Harvard University Press, 1970), and my own *Transformations of Romanticism in Yeats, Eliot, and Stevens* (Chicago: University of Chicago Press, 1976).

3. *Samuel Butler's Notebooks*, ed. Geoffrey Keynes and Brian Hill (London: Jonathan Cape, 1951), pp. 77–78. Butler's conjunction of Blake, Dante, and Tennyson is echoed in various ways by the essays that follow in the present volume.

4. Carol T. Christ, *Victorian and Modern Poetics* (Chicago: University of Chicago Press, 1984). Robert Langbaum's classic *The Poetry of Experience* (1957; rptd. New York: W. W. Norton, 1963) remains central to discussions of Victorian and modern poetry.

5. *Selected Letters of Ezra Pound 1907–1941*, ed. D. D. Paige (New York: New Directions, 1971), p. 218.

6. Browning suggests that just as the ancients exploited purple dye from the murex (a shellfish) but failed to reward its discoverer, so did Victorian poetasters attain a popularity and wealth which in his lifetime eluded the true innovator, Keats. See my "'What Porridge Had John Keats?': Pound's 'L'Art' and Browning's 'Popularity,'" *Paideuma* 10 (1981): 303–6.

7. T. S. Eliot, *Selected Essays* (New York: Harcourt, Brace & World, 1964), p. 295; A. Walton Litz, "'That Strange Abstraction, "Nature"': T. S. Eliot's Victorian Inheritance," in *Nature and the Victorian Imagination*, ed. U. C. Knoepflmacher and G. B. Tennyson (Berkeley: University of California Press, 1977), pp. 470–88.

8. *The Variorum Edition of the Poems of W. B. Yeats*, ed. Peter Allt and Russell K. Alspach (New York: Macmillan, 1966), p. 605.

9. *Uncollected Prose by W. B. Yeats*, vol. 1, ed. John P. Frayne (New York: Columbia University Press, 1970), p. 277.

10. *Letters to the New Island*, ed. Horace Reynolds (Cambridge: Harvard University Press, 1934, rptd. 1970), pp. 74 and 174 (italics mine). The first quotation appeared in the Boston *Pilot* and the second in the *Providence Sunday Journal*. An expanded, corrected, and annotated edition of *Letters to the New Island*, edited by George Bornstein and Hugh Witemeyer, is forthcoming from Macmillan as part of the new Collected Edition of the Works of W. B. Yeats.

11. See Longfellow's 1832 review of a new printing of Sidney's *Apology for Poetry*, reprinted in *The Native Muse: Theories of American Literature*, vol. 1, ed. Richard Ruland (New York: E. P. Dutton, 1972), p. 257; Whitman's editorial in the *Brooklyn Eagle* for 10 February 1847, quoted in Perry Miller, *The Raven and the Whale: The War of Words and Wits in the Era of Poe and Melville* (New York: Harcourt, Brace, 1956), p. 187; and Lowell's "On a Certain Condescension in Foreigners," in *The Writings of James Russell Lowell* (Boston: Houghton Mifflin, 1891), vol. 3, p. 252.

12. *Letters to the New Island*, p. 76.

13. Robert Weisbuch, *Atlantic Double-Cross: American Literature and British Influence in the Age of Emerson* (Chicago: University of Chicago Press, 1986), pp. ix–x. The quotation from Willis and Morris appears on p. 5. I am grateful to Weisbuch for a series of discussions of Anglo-American literary influence extending over the past several years and for guiding me to several of the quotations in the present paragraph.

14. Wallace Stevens, "A Mythology Reflects Its Region," in *The Palm at the End of the Mind* (New York: Vintage Books, 1972), p. 398.

15. *Autobiographies* (London: Macmillan, 1966), pp. 193–94.

16. See Fraistat's important monograph, *The Poem and the Book: Interpreting Collections of Romantic Poetry* (Chapel Hill: University of North Carolina Press, 1985), and his broader collection of essays by various hands, *Poems in Their Place: The Intertextuality and Order of Poetic Collections* (Chapel Hill: University of North Carolina Press, 1986). I have drawn heavily on Fraistat's work for some of the information in the present paragraph.

17. *Literary Essays of Ezra Pound* (New York: New Directions, 1968), pp. 418–22.

18. Fraistat, *Poems in Their Place*, pp. 3–4.

19. I explore this topic in more detail in a forthcoming essay, "Remaking Himself: Yeats's Revisions of His Early Canon," originally delivered as a paper at the Modern Language Association meeting, December 1986.

20. *A Vision* (New York: Macmillan, 1966), p. 24.

CHAPTER 2

1. John Forster's review appeared in *The Examiner* for 26 November 1842 and is conveniently reprinted in *Browning: The Critical Heritage*, ed. Boyd Litzinger and Donald Smalley (New York: Barnes and Noble, 1970), pp. 82–84. The remark cited is on p. 83.

2. William E. Harrold's *The Variance and the Unity: A Study of the Complementary*

Poems of Robert Browning (Athens: Ohio University Press, 1973), the most detailed study to date, briefly discusses four of the groupings from *Dramatic Lyrics* but concentrates on later poems. Harrold's commitment to Gestalt and Jungian psychology, his focus on pairs rather than volumes, and some of his individual readings (e.g., of Porphyria's lover as a Neoplatonist) lead him to conclusions quite different from mine. Nancy B. Rich has some comments on "Madhouse Cells" in the course of her "New Perspective on the Companion Poems of Robert Browning," *Victorian Newsletter* 36 (1969): 5–9. Lawrence Poston III, in "Browning Rearranges Browning," *Studies in Browning and His Circle* 2 (1974): 39–54, studies the 1863 rearrangement as "a kind of backward look" over Browning's career. Like Harrold, Poston denies an overall significance to the early volumes but does include helpful remarks on two pairings and two more individual poems. More recently, Daniel Karlin in "Browning's Paired Poems," *Essays in Criticism* 31 (1981): 210–27, deals with a few poems from 1845 onwards.

    3. On *Dramatis Personae* see Lawrence Poston III, *Loss and Gain: An Essay on Browning's Dramatis Personae*, University of Nebraska Studies No. 48 (Lincoln: University of Nebraska Press, 1974); and Thomas Wyly, "Unity and Design in Browning's *Dramatis Personae*," *Revue des Langues Vivantes* 43 (1977): 38–53.

    4. The pamphlet itself lacks a table of contents; I have simply listed the titles in the order in which they appear. Browning kept the same ordering but removed most of the titular pairings for the 1849 collected edition *Dramatic Romances and Lyrics*, which combined the 1842 *Dramatic Lyrics* with the 1845 *Dramatic Romances and Lyrics*. In 1863 he redistributed the poems from the first two volumes and *Men and Women* but confusingly kept the old titles as categories. Basic accounts of the later versions can be found in William Clyde DeVane, *A Browning Handbook* (New York: Appleton-Century-Crofts, 1955), pp. 102–4, 150–53, and 205–8; in the text and notes to volumes 3 and 5 of *The Complete Works of Robert Browning*, ed. Roma A. King, Jr., et al. (Athens: Ohio University Press, 1969–); and in the notes to *Robert Browning: The Poems*, ed. John Pettigrew, supplemented and completed by Thomas J. Collins (New Haven: Yale University Press, 1981), vol. 1. Quotations in the present chapter come from the Pettigrew-Collins volume because of its accessibility and reliability; most of the poems are short enough for quotations to be located readily, but I have supplied line numbers within parentheses in my text for citations from the few lengthy poems of the volume. For those few cases dealing with the original wording, I have followed the Ohio Browning, giving volume and page numbers.

    5. See Mrs. Sutherland Orr, *Life and Letters of Robert Browning*, New Edition (London: Smith, Elder & Co., 1908), p. 122.

    6. DeVane, *Browning Handbook*, p. 106, assigns composition of "Cavalier Tunes" to the summer of 1842. W. Hall Griffin and Harry Christopher Minchin in their standard *The Life of Robert Browning* (London: Methuen, 1910), p. 73, date composition of "Madhouse Cells" as April–May 1834, but later commentators have been skeptical; Collins, *Robert Browning: The Poems*, vol. 1, p. 1084, makes a case for 1835. The pair was first published in *The Monthly Repository* for January 1836.

    7. Poston, "Browning Rearranges Browning," p. 41.

    8. See Browning's letter to Alfred Domett, the model for Waring, on 22 May 1842, in which he announces his intention to "print a few songs and small poems which Moxon advised me to do for popularity's sake!" The letter is included in F. G. Kenyon,

ed., *Robert Browning and Alfred Domett* (New York: E. P. Dutton & Co., 1906), pp. 33–39; the quotation is on p. 36.

9. M. H. Abrams, "Structure and Style in the Greater Romantic Lyric," in *From Sensibility to Romanticism*, ed. Frederick W. Hilles and Harold Bloom (New York: Oxford University Press, 1965), pp. 527–60. I first argued for adapting Abrams's schema to description-vision-evaluation in *Transformations of Romanticism in Yeats, Eliot, and Stevens* (Chicago: University of Chicago Press, 1976), passim, and apply it to Browning's "Pictor Ignotus" in the next chapter of the present volume.

10. John V. Hagopian in "The Mask of Browning's Countess Gismond," *Philological Quarterly* 40 (1961): 153–55, and John W. Tilton and R. Dale Tuttle in "A New Reading of 'Count Gismond,'" *Studies in Philology* 59 (1962): 83–95, argue for a negative view of the Countess but go too far, as perhaps does Michael Timko in the other direction in his exasperated rejoinder, "Ah, Did You Once See Browning Plain?" *Studies in English Literature* 6 (1966): 731–42. Agreeing with some of Timko's reservations and with his rejection of the attempt to paint Count Gismond as tyrant in Sister Marcella M. Holloway's "A Further Reading of 'Count Gismond,'" *Studies in Philology* 60 (1963): 549–53, I would take a middle ground and maintain that the evidence of the Countess's duplicity is neither definitive nor negligible, and that Browning exploits the resultant uncertainty in his subtle psychological probing. Harrold in *The Variance and the Unity* assumes the worst about the Countess; his passing remarks on the time sequence (p. 39) are suggestive.

11. In the often-quoted phrase of Browning's friend Joseph Arnould, "Waring" presents a "fancy portrait of a very dear friend"; see Kenyon, *Robert Browning and Alfred Domett*, p. 62. On the proof-sheets at Harvard, Browning wrote "Alfred Domett or" above the printed title. Browning borrowed the name Waring itself from a diplomatic messenger he met in Russia.

12. For a helpful discussion relating the poem to Browning's own artistic problems and biographical dilemmas, see John F. McCarthy, "Browning's 'Waring': The Real Subject of the 'Fancy Portrait,'" *Victorian Poetry* 9 (1971): 371–82. McCarthy sees the poem as "an ironic treatment of the early Browning's favorite theme—the dilemma of the non-communicating artist-prophet"; I am unable, however, to share his view of Waring as "hard-boiled."

13. For example, Lord Malmesbury wrote in his *Memoirs of an Ex-Minister* (London: Longmans, Green, and Co., 1884) that she "was said at the time to be the cause of more than one inflammable victim languishing in prison for having too openly admired this royal coquette, whose manners with men foretold her future life after her marriage to old Ferdinand" (1:30).

14. Other passages pertaining to Elective Affinities in Browning include lines 25–30 of "The Statue and the Bust" and lines 1162–75 of "Caponsacchi" in *The Ring and the Book*. In his brief "Browning's 'Cristina,'" *Explicator* 2 (1943–44), Item 16, Clyde S. Kilby helpfully corrects traditional commentary by suggesting that the speaker is "eccentric."

15. The headnote is conveniently reprinted in the Pettigrew-Collins edition, *Robert Browning: The Poems*, vol. 1, p. 1084.

16. See DeVane, *Browning Handbook*, pp. 126–27, and the Ohio Browning 3:384.

17. According to Mrs. Orr, *Life and Letters*, p. 122, the poem "was added to the

Dramatic Lyrics, because some columns of that number of *Bells and Pomegranates* still required filling." Pettigrew and Collins, *Robert Browning: The Poems,* vol. 1, p. 1085, note that "The Pied Piper" appears in the second set of proofs but not in the first.
    18. See Arthur N. Kincaid and Peter W. M. Blayney, "A Book of Browning's and His 'Essay on Chatterton,'" *Browning Society Notes* 2 (1972): 11–25, esp. p. 23.
    19. For more extended treatments of the artist theme in "The Pied Piper," see Milton Millhauser, "Poet and Burgher: A Comic Variation on a Serious Theme," *Victorian Poetry* 7 (1969): 163–68, and Wolfgang Francke, "Browning's 'Pied Piper of Hamelin': Two Levels of Meaning," *ARIEL: A Review of International English Literature* 2 (1971): 90–97. Francke confuses *Dramatic Lyrics* (1842) with the 1849 collection.
    20. Francke, "Browning's 'Pied Piper,'" pp. 96–97.

CHAPTER 3

    1. William Clyde DeVane took a favorable view of the pictor in *A Browning Handbook* (New York: F. S. Crofts, 1935), pp. 140–41. Paul F. Jamieson's counterargument in "Browning's 'Pictor Ignotus, Florence, 15—,'" *Explicator* 11 (1952), Item 8, partially convinced even DeVane in the revised 1955 handbook. J. B. Bullen's proposal of the identification with Fra Bartolommeo in "Browning's 'Pictor Ignotus' and Vasari's 'Life of Fra Bartolommeo di San Marco,'" *Review of English Studies* 23 (1972): 313–19, has the support of Ian Jack in *Browning's Major Poetry* (London: Oxford University Press, 1973), pp. 208–13; but the observations of Michael H. Bright in "Browning's Celebrated Pictor Ignotus," *English Language Notes* 13 (1976): 192–94, seem to me more convincing.
    2. For a review of some of this scholarship, see my *Transformations of Romanticism in Yeats, Eliot, and Stevens* (Chicago: University of Chicago Press, 1976), ch. 1.
    3. *The Complete Works of Robert Browning,* ed. Roma A. King, Jr., et al. (Athens: Ohio University Press, 1969–), I, 65. Hereafter cited within the text by volume and page number.
    4. For a fine discussion of this and related forms, see A. Dwight Culler, "Monodrama and the Dramatic Monologue," *PMLA* 90 (1975): 366–85; Culler has some especially pertinent remarks on the distinction between the two forms on p. 382.
    5. My argument about the structure revealed by mental action coheres with Michael Bright's observation on argumentative logic in the poem in his helpful essay, "Browning's 'Pictor Ignotus': An Interpretation," *Studies in Browning and His Circle* 4 (Spring 1976): 53–61. Bright sees the monologue as following "the pattern of a formal syllogism in that the three sections are governed respectively by 'if' (implied), 'But,' and 'Wherefore'" (pp. 54–55).
    6. For relation of the poem to the essay on Shelley, see Fred Kaplan, *Miracles of Rare Device: The Poet's Sense of Self in Nineteenth-Century Poetry* (Detroit: Wayne State University Press, 1972), pp. 110–15.
    7. *The Poetry of Browning: A Critical Introduction* (London: Methuen, 1970), p. 266n.
    8. Herbert F. Tucker, Jr., *Browning's Beginnings: The Art of Disclosure* (Minneapolis: University of Minnesota Press, 1980), p. 167.

CHAPTER 4

1. Robert Browning, *The Poems*, ed. John Pettigrew, supplemented and completed by Thomas J. Collins (New Haven: Yale University Press, 1981), vol. 1, p. 777. All further quotations from Browning are from this edition.

2. *The Poems and Fables of John Dryden*, ed. James Kinsley (London: Oxford University Press, 1962), p. 489. W. Jackson Bate has made splendid use of Dryden's lines in his *The Burden of the Past and the English Poet* (Cambridge: The Belknap Press of Harvard University Press, 1970).

3. Matthew Arnold, *On the Classical Tradition*, ed. R. H. Super (Ann Arbor: University of Michigan Press, 1960), p. 9.

4. M. H. Abrams, "Structure and Style in the Greater Romantic Lyric," in *From Sensibility to Romanticism*, ed. Frederick W. Hilles and Harold Bloom (New York: Oxford University Press, 1965), pp. 527–60.

5. *The Poems of Tennyson*, ed. Christopher Ricks (New York: Norton, 1972), pp. 946–47. All further quotations from Tennyson are from this edition.

6. Hallam Tennyson, *Alfred Lord Tennyson: A Memoir* (New York: Macmillan, 1897), vol. 1, p. 320.

7. See the textual notes in Ricks's edition, pp. 946–47, and in *In Memoriam*, ed. Robert H. Ross (New York: Norton, 1973), p. 61.

8. *Poetry and Criticism of Matthew Arnold*, ed. A. Dwight Culler (Boston: Houghton Mifflin, 1961), p. 148.

9. Joseph Glanvil, *The Vanity of Dogmatizing*, ed. Moody E. Prior (New York: Published for The Facsimile Text Society by Columbia University Press, 1931), p. 197.

10. Browning, *The Poems*, p. 722.

11. *Letters of Robert Browning*, ed. Thurman L. Hood (New Haven: Yale University Press, 1933), p. 235.

12. Browning used that phrase in the 1837 Preface to *Strafford*. See *The Complete Works of Robert Browning*, ed. Roma A. King, Jr., et al. (Athens: Ohio University Press, 1970), II, 9.

13. T. S. Eliot, *Collected Poems 1909–1962* (New York: Harcourt, Brace & World, 1963), p. 29.

14. W. B. Yeats, *The Poems: A New Edition*, ed. Richard J. Finneran (New York: Macmillan, 1983), p. 177.

CHAPTER 5

1. *The Variorum Edition of the Poems of W. B. Yeats*, ed. Peter Allt and Russell K. Alspach (New York: Macmillan, 1957), p. 480. Hereafter cited in the text as VP followed by page number. Cf. Yeats's note to *The Winding Stair*: "In this book and elsewhere I have used towers, and one tower in particular, as symbols and have compared their winding stairs to the philosophical gyres, but it is hardly necessary to interpret what comes from the main track of thought and expression. Shelley uses towers constantly as symbols" (VP 831). Yeats had traced Shelley's use of towers in "The Philosophy of Shelley's Poetry."

2. I have already given my views on Yeats's early romanticism in *Yeats and Shelley*

(Chicago: University of Chicago Press, 1970); Harold Bloom uses a different approach to arrive at many similar and some quite different views in his *Yeats* (New York: Oxford University Press, 1970). The two books are in part complementary.

3. Cf. "pictures of the mind" in "In Memory of Eva Gore-Booth and Con Markiewicz" (VP 475).

4. Quoted in M. H. Abrams, "Structure and Style in the Greater Romantic Lyric," in *From Sensibility to Romanticism: Essays Presented to Frederick A. Pottle,* ed. Frederick W. Hilles and Harold Bloom (New York: Oxford University Press, 1965), p. 532. Ellipses mine.

5. A. Norman Jeffares has even suggested a possible echo in "The Tower" of Blake on bodily decay; see his *A Commentary on the Collected Poems of W. B. Yeats* (Stanford: Stanford University Press, 1968), p. 258.

6. W. B. Yeats, *Memoirs,* ed. Denis Donoghue (London: Macmillan, 1972), p. 133. See pp. 33 and 84 for Yeats's conception of his youthful love as romantic.

7. *Essays and Introductions* (New York: Macmillan, 1961), p. 291.

8. Horton's contemplation of an image links this poem to the more recondite "Phases of the Moon" (1919), where the creatures of the full moon, or phase fifteen, fix the mind's eye "upon images that once were thought" (VP 375).

9. *Mythologies* (London: Macmillan, 1962), pp. 345–46.

10. In *The English Review* and *The Little Review,* 1918.

11. It moves out-in-out, with a parallel present-past-present pattern.

12. See Jon Stallworthy, *Between the Lines: Yeats's Poetry in the Making* (Oxford: Clarendon Press, 1963), p. 17.

13. This phrase comes from Yeats's own note to "The Second Coming" (VP 825).

14. *Yeats,* p. 320.

15. Margaret Rudd first noticed this in her *Divided Image: A Study of William Blake and W. B. Yeats* (London: Routledge & Kegan Paul, 1953), p. 119. There is an interesting discussion in Bloom, *Yeats,* p. 319.

16. In *Yeats and Shelley,* pp. 195–98.

17. VP 425. See VP 827 for Yeats's note.

18. Yeats's prose draft for the poem began: "Describe house in first stanza." Parkinson has a valuable discussion of the evolution of the poem, in *W. B. Yeats: The Later Poetry* (Berkeley: University of California Press, 1964), pp. 80–81, followed by a longer one of "Among School Children."

19. Jeffares compares Pythagoras's use of a swallow image; see *A Commentary,* p. 344.

CHAPTER 6

1. W. B. Yeats, *Autobiographies* (London: Macmillan, 1966), pp. 114–15. Hereafter cited as A followed by page number. Yeats's response was not unusual. In *Rossetti* (London: Duckworth, 1902), p. 38, Ford Madox Ford took a more guarded view of the important effect of this picture: "The fact remains that, after having seen the picture, this episode of Dante's life must be visualized by men of our time, in a place and with figures like those of Rossetti's. And this implies a great deal."

2. See, for example, the discussion of the *Vita Nuova* in T. S. Eliot, *Selected Essays* (New York: Harcourt, Brace & World, 1964), p. 235. Eliot repeatedly contrasts Dante and the Romantics.

3. As quoted by F. P. Wilson, "A Supplement to Toynbee's *Dante in English Literature,*" *Italian Studies* 3 (1946): 50–64. Wilson's work supplements Paget Toynbee's immense *Dante in English Literature from Chaucer to Cary,* 2 vols. (London: Methuen, 1909), which reprints every mention of Dante he could find by an English man of letters. For the convenience of the reader, I have cited Wilson and Toynbee in preference to a variety of separate texts.

4. Toynbee, vol. 1, p. 255.

5. Toynbee, vol. 1, p. 341.

6. See Oswald Doughty, "Dante and the English Romantic Poets," *English Miscellany* 2 (1951): 136. Byron was less enthusiastic. For Blake's reading of Cary and knowledge of Dante, see Albert S. Roe, *Blake's Illustrations to the Divine Comedy* (Princeton: Princeton University Press, 1953), pp. 4, 6, 30–34.

7. E. H. Plumptre, trans., *The Commedia and Canzoniere of Dante Alighieri,* 2 vols. (London: Wm. Ibister, 1887), vol. 2, p. 440. Plumptre was Dean of Wells and himself a translator of Dante.

8. W. B. Yeats, *Mythologies* (London: Macmillan, 1962), p. 329. Hereafter cited as M followed by page number. Yeats knew other translations as well. All quotations from Dante in the present essay come from versions known to Yeats or, where certain identification is lacking, at least from those accessible to him.

9. Charles Lancelot Shadwell, trans., *The Purgatory of Dante Alighieri* (London: Macmillan, 1892), p. xiv; hereafter cited as Shadwell followed by page number. Other quotations in this paragraph may be found on pp. xvii, xix, xxiii. Voltaire had written in the *Dictionnaire Philosophique* that "sa réputation s'affermira toujours parcequ'on ne le lit guère." In William J. De Sua, *Dante into English: A Study of the Translations of the Divine Comedy in Britain and America* (Chapel Hill: University of North Carolina Press, 1964), p. 77, De Sua calls Shadwell "the best poetic translation of the late 19th century," but in Gilbert F. Cunningham, *The Divine Comedy into English: A Critical Bibliography 1782–1900* (Edinburgh: Oliver and Boyd, 1965), p. 186, Cunningham cautions that Shadwell's stanzas "form a very poor guide for the reader whose knowledge of the *Comedy* can be obtained only from an English translation." Citations from Cary's translation in this essay come from Henry Francis Cary, trans. and ed., *The Vision; or Hell, Purgatory, and Paradise, of Dante Alighieri* (London: George Bell and Sons, 1889); hereafter cited as Cary followed by page number.

10. *Uncollected Prose by W. B. Yeats,* ed. John P. Frayne (New York: Columbia University Press, 1970), vol. 1, pp. 251–52; hereafter cited as Uncoll followed by page number. As usual when mentioning Dante, Yeats went on to discuss romantic poets, in this case Blake and Shelley.

11. W. B. Yeats, *Essays and Introductions* (New York: Macmillan, 1961), p. 140. Hereafter cited as E&I followed by page number.

12. *The Works of William Blake: Poetic, Symbolic, and Critical,* ed. Edwin John Ellis and William Butler Yeats, 3 vols. (London: Bernard Quaritch, 1893), vol. 1, pp. 137–40; *Poems of William Blake,* ed. W. B. Yeats (London: Lawrence and Bullen, 1893), p. xlvi.

13. The eight included the watercolors of *The Passing of Dante and Virgil through the Portico of Hell; Angry Spirits Fighting in the Waters of the Styx; Antaeus Setting Virgil and Dante upon the Verge of Cocytus; Dante and Uberti; Dante and Virgil Climbing to the Foot of the Mountain of Purgatory; Dante, Virgil and Statius; The Car of Beatrice;* and John Linnell's tracing of Blake's drawing for *The Car Following the Seven Candlesticks.* For Yeats's projected use of the Paolo and Francesca as frontispiece to *Ideas of Good and Evil,* see *The Letters of W. B. Yeats,* ed. Allan Wade (London: Rubert Hart-Davis, 1954), p. 377; hereafter cited as Lett followed by page number.

14. Arthur Symons, *Savoy* 8 (December 1896): 92.

15. Yeats, *Uncollected Prose,* p. 141. The following quotations come from pp. 284, 328.

16. *The Variorum Edition of the Poems of W. B. Yeats,* ed. Peter Allt and Russell K. Alspach (New York: Macmillan, 1966), p. 125. Hereafter cited as VP followed by page number.

17. *The Variorum Edition of the Plays of W. B. Yeats,* ed. Russell K. Alspach (New York: Macmillan, 1966), p. 168.

18. W. B. Yeats, *Explorations* (New York: Macmillan, [1963]), p. 190. Hereafter cited as E followed by page number.

19. W. B. Yeats, *Memoirs,* ed. Denis Donoghue (London: Macmillan, 1972), p. 248. Cf. *Memoirs,* p. 247: "Dante is said to have unified Italy," and E&I 341.

20. Allen R. Grossman, *Poetic Knowledge in the Early Yeats: A Study of "The Wind Among the Reeds"* (Charlottesville: University of Virginia Press, 1969).

21. *W. B. Yeats and T. Sturge Moore: Their Correspondence 1901–1937,* ed. Ursula Bridge (London: Routledge & Kegan Paul, 1953), p. 38. Since the subject of Yeats's letter is his hawk symbol, I have added bird to the list.

22. Thomas Vance, "Dante, Yeats, and Unity of Being," *Shenandoah* 17 (1965): 83.

23. Yeats knew Boccaccio's life of Dante; for example, he quotes his remark that "Always both in youth and maturity [Dante] found room among his virtues for lechery" (M 330). In the same place Yeats quoted Rossetti's translation of Guido Cavalcanti's reproach to Dante. The conjunction of an "apple" on a "bough" out of reach occurs in Shadwell's version of *Purgatory* 27, "That apple sweet, from bough to bough / By man so dearly sought" (Shadwell 407). I owe this last point to my student, David Spurr, who has written a useful essay on "A Celtic Commedia: Dante in Yeats's Poetry," *Rackham Literary Studies* (Spring 1977): 99–116.

24. E 250. Cf. W. B. Yeats, *A Vision* (New York: Macmillan, 1958), p. 289; hereafter cited as V followed by page number. All quotations from *A Vision* come from that text, except for passages deleted from the original 1925 version (London: T. Werner Laurie); hereafter cited as 1925V followed by page number.

25. For other instances see E&I 483, 509; E 356; A 190; and V 258, 291.

26. Elizabeth Price Sayer, trans., *Il Convito: The Banquet of Dante Alighieri* (London: George Routledge and Sons, 1887), pp. 126, 156.

27. George Bornstein, *Yeats and Shelley* (Chicago: University of Chicago Press, 1970), pp. 199–218; pp. 218–22 discuss the relationship between Shelley and Yeats as critics of Dante. The quotation about Shelley shaping Yeats's life is from E&I 424.

28. Yeats also compares Dante and Villon in E&I 349 and A 310. Hugh Witemeyer and I have discussed his view of Villon in more detail in "From *Villian* to Visionary:

Pound and Yeats on Villon," *Comparative Literature* 19 (Fall 1967): 308–20. For other references to Dante and Balzac than those below, see E&I 446 and E 269, 277.

29. Besides those discussed elsewhere in this essay, the "emerald eyes" of *The Mask* may derive from those of Beatrice in *Purgatory* 31, the butterflies of *Blood and the Moon* from that in *Purgatory* 10, the sighing in *News for the Delphic Oracle* from that in *Inferno* 4, the "water, herb and solitary prayer" of *Ribh at the Tomb of Baile and Aillinn* from the end of *Purgatory* 22, and Rocky Face of *The Gyres* from the figure of Dante among others. *Why Should Not Old Men Be Mad* refers to "a girl that knew all Dante once." David R. Clark, *W. B. Yeats and the Theatre of Desolate Reality* (Dublin: Dolmen Press, 1965), pp. 21–25, has suggested that the plays *The Dreaming of the Bones, The Words upon the Window-pane,* and *Purgatory* all draw upon the Paolo and Francesca episode. Giorgio Melchiori devotes considerable space to the relation of the story originally known as "The Vision of O'Sullivan the Red" to Dante in his helpful survey, "Yeats and Dante," *English Miscellany* 19 (1968): 153–79. In the chapter on Yeats in his recent *Dante and English Poetry: Shelley to T. S. Eliot* (Cambridge: Cambridge University Press, 1983), Steve Ellis traces Yeats's fondness for the adjective "pearl-pale" back to Rossetti's description of Beatrice. Finally, Tilottama Rajan in "The Romantic Backgrounds of Yeats's Use of Dante in 'Ego Dominus Tuus,'" *Yeats Eliot Review* 7 (1982): 120–22, suggests that Carlyle may be an important filter for the impact of Dante on that poem.

30. Yeats had gotten into trouble by using Christian symbols in *The Countess Cathleen,* which we have already seen drew upon Dante. Recalling the protests that the play was anti-Catholic, Yeats wrote that "in using what I considered traditional symbols I forgot that in Ireland they are not symbols but realities" (A 416).

31. Because of its similarity to Yeats in phrasing, I have quoted here from William Michael Rossetti's translation, *The Comedy of Dante Alighieri: Part I—The Hell* (London: Macmillan, 1865), p. 4. For the early drafts see Jon Stallworthy, *Between the Lines: W. B. Yeats's Poetry in the Making* (Oxford: Clarendon Press, 1963), ch. 6. The following quotation about flames comes from p. 123.

32. F. A. C. Wilson, *W. B. Yeats and Tradition* (New York: Macmillan, 1958), p. 246; T. R. Henn, *The Lonely Tower: Studies in the Poetry of W. B. Yeats* (London: Methuen, 1965), p. 338. Helen Vendler suggests a syntactic parallel between *Inferno* 15 and the prose draft of Yeats's poem, in *Yeats's Vision and the Later Plays* (Cambridge: Harvard University Press, 1963), p. 247. For the prose version of the poem, see Dorothy Wellesley, ed., *Letters on Poetry from W. B. Yeats to Dorothy Wellesley* (London: Oxford University Press, 1964), p. 193.

33. The list is reprinted in Curtis Bradford, "The Order of Yeats's *Last Poems*," *Modern Language Notes* 76 (1961): 515–16. Richard J. Finneran's recent *The Poems of W. B. Yeats: A New Edition* (New York: Macmillan, 1983) properly follows the order of Yeats's own list.

CHAPTER 7

1. *Autobiographies* (London: Macmillan, 1966), pp. 66–67; hereafter cited as Au followed by page number.

2. I mean here not only Yeats's well-known tendency to see himself as a "last romantic," particularly in terms of Blake and Shelley, but also his habit of viewing other poets he admired (like Dante) as in some way romantic. An earlier and shorter version of the present essay appears as the "Yeats" entry in *The Spenser Encyclopedia*, forthcoming from University of Toronto Press.

3. See Richard Ellmann, *Yeats: The Man and the Masks* (New York: Macmillan, 1948), pp. 28–29. The manuscripts are from the collection of Michael Yeats, for whose cooperation I am grateful, and are currently housed in the National Library of Ireland. Because the manuscripts are confusing, the identification in the text of the two following quotations by stanza number needs a clarification. The stanza 4 containing the first quotation has been renumbered as 5; the stanza 21 containing the second quotation is one of two consecutive stanzas bearing that number.

4. For a full transcription of the drafts, see W. B. Yeats, *The Early Poetry, Volume I: Mosada and The Island of Statues, Manuscript Materials*, ed. George Bornstein (Ithaca: Cornell University Press, 1987).

5. *The Variorum Edition of the Poems of W. B. Yeats*, ed. Peter Allt and Russell K. Alspach (New York: Macmillan, corrected 3rd printing, 1966), p. 7; hereafter cited as VP followed by page number. The description of Belphoebe's speech is from *The Faerie Queene*, Book II, canto iii, stanza 24.

6. National Library of Ireland, Ms. 3726. A full transcription of the entire draft will be included in W. B. Yeats, *The Early Poetry, Volume II*, ed. George Bornstein, forthcoming from Cornell University Press. Victorian editions of Spenser frequently followed similar spellings to Yeats's. The only surviving one from Yeats's own library early enough for him to have read by the time of composition of *Oisin*—Roden Noel's *The Poems of Spenser* (London: Walter Scott, 1886)—uses "honny" in the Belphoebe passage, as does J. Payne Collier's edition described below, which first appeared in 1862 but which Yeats seems to have acquired only in 1892.

7. *The Letters of W. B. Yeats*, ed. Allan Wade (London: Rupert Hart-Davis, 1954), p. 365; hereafter cited as L followed by page number. For a survey of Yeats's letters referring to the edition, see A. G. Stock, "Yeats on Spenser," in *In Excited Reverie: A Centenary Tribute to William Butler Yeats, 1865–1939*, ed. A. Norman Jeffares and K. G. W. Cross (London: Macmillan; New York: St. Martin's, 1965), pp. 93–101.

8. "Introduction" to *Poems of Spenser*, ed. W. B. Yeats (Edinburgh: T. C. & E. C. Jack, 1906), p. xliv. For the reader's convenience, I cite further references to this essay from the more accessible text in *Essays and Introductions* (New York: Macmillan, 1961), hereafter identified as E&I, which differs from the 1906 volume in minor ways but not in the passages that I cite.

9. The volumes themselves are part of Yeats's library in the collection of Anne Yeats, whose kindness in helping with the present article as well as other work has been extraordinary. Perhaps the greatest number of markings and marginalia concern problems of selection for Yeats's own edition; I have focused here on more substantive comments instead. The pencil inscription on the flyleaf of volume I—"W. B. Yeats / March—1892 / A. G."—in Lady Gregory's hand remains something of a mystery owing to the date. Citations of Yeats's marginalia to this edition will be indicated by the volume number in roman numerals followed by the page number in arabic numerals, enclosed within parentheses in the text.

10. I owe this observation to T. McAlindon's generally helpful article "Yeats and the English Renaissance," *PMLA* 82 (1967): 157–69.

11. The notepaper is headed "Coole Park, / Gort, / Co. Galway" and is tucked between pages 386 and 387 of volume IV of Yeats's copy of Collier's edition. I have replaced Yeats's period with an interrogation mark to clarify the sense.

CHAPTER 8

1. *The Variorum Edition of the Poems of W. B. Yeats*, ed. Peter Allt and Russell K. Alspach (New York: Macmillan, rev. 3rd printing, 1966), pp. 491–92. Hereafter cited as VP followed by page number.

2. The best general recent study is Carol Christ's *Victorian and Modern Poetics* (Chicago: University of Chicago Press, 1984). For a suggestive reappraisal in relation to T. S. Eliot, see A. Walton Litz, "'That Strange Abstraction, "Nature"'': T. S. Eliot's Victorian Inheritance," in *Nature and the Victorian Imagination*, ed. U. C. Knoepflmacher and G. B. Tennyson (Berkeley: University of California Press, 1977), pp. 470–88. I return to Pound's relation to Browning in the next chapter.

3. "The Music of Poetry" (1942), in *On Poetry and Poets* (New York: Farrar, Straus & Giroux, 1961), pp. 17–18.

4. W. B. Yeats, ed., *The Oxford Book of Modern Verse* (New York: Oxford University Press, 1936), p. v; hereafter cited in the text as Oxf followed by page number. Cf. Yeats's letter to Sturge Moore on this point in *W. B. Yeats and T. Sturge Moore: Their Correspondence, 1901–1937*, ed. Ursula Bridge (London: Routledge & Kegan Paul, 1953), p. 182, hereafter cited as LTSM followed by page number; and "Modern Poetry: A Broadcast," in *Essays and Introductions* (New York: Macmillan, 1961), p. 491, hereafter cited as E&I followed by page number.

5. E&I 190–91. For the passage in the review of Symons's *Amoris Victima*, see *Uncollected Prose by W. B. Yeats*, vol. 2, ed. John P. Frayne and Colton Johnson (New York: Columbia University Press, 1976), pp. 39–40. Hereafter cited as UP2 followed by page number. Cf. E&I 113, 163, 192, 495; UP2 91; and *Autobiographies* (London: Macmillan, 1966), p. 167, hereafter cited as Au followed by page number, for similar views.

6. UP2 88–89. See *Uncollected Prose by W. B. Yeats*, vol. 1, ed. John P. Frayne (New York: Columbia University Press, 1970), pp. 276–79, hereafter cited as UP1 followed by page number; UP2 34 and 130; Au 484 and 489–90; and the lecture "Friends of My Youth," in *Yeats and the Theatre*, ed. Robert O'Driscoll and Lorna Reynolds (London: Macmillan, 1975), p. 28, for other important references to Hallam's essay.

7. For Yeats's critique of syntax and speech in Tennyson and Browning, see Richard Fallis's "Language and Rhythm in Poetry: A Previously Unpublished Essay by W. B. Yeats" (*Shenandoah*, vol. 26, no. 4 [Summer 1975]: 77–79), where Yeats declares *In Memoriam* "detestable because of its syntax." Fallis utilizes Yeats's unfinished remarks during his brief discussion of Tennyson in "Yeats and the Reinterpretation of Victorian Poetry" (*Victorian Poetry* 14 [1976]: 93), which offers helpful short accounts of Yeats's response to Tennyson, Arnold, Browning, Hardy, Hopkins, Morris, and others.

8. Matthew Arnold, *Lectures and Essays in Criticism,* ed. R. H. Super (Ann Arbor: University of Michigan Press, 1962), p. 390.

9. All quotations from the *Death of Oenone* review may be found in UP1 251–54.

10. The later Tennyson pleased Yeats in one other way: His "The Voyage of Maeldune" sanctioned by its example the use of Celtic materials in modern poetry. See UP1 286 and *The Letters of W. B. Yeats,* ed. Allan Wade (London: Rupert Hart-Davis, 1954), pp. 105–6, hereafter cited as L followed by page number.

11. For another example of this change, compare a 1914 condemnation, "One may admire Tennyson, but one cannot read him" (*The Egoist,* vol. 1, no. 3 [2 February 1914]: 57), with the more implicitly favorable remark to T. Sturge Moore in 1929, "I can no more expect you to acknowledge virtue in Hegel than Ezra Pound to acknowledge it in Tennyson" (LTSM 153). Two years later, Yeats responded to an interviewer's query about what Victorian poet he admired: "Browning, of course, and if I live another ten years I shall admire Tennyson again" (Louise Morgan, *Writers at Work* [London: Chatto & Windus, 1931], p. 8).

12. Au 342. Cf. UP1 399, UP2 413, E&I 270, and Oxf ix.

13. W. B. Yeats, *Memoirs,* ed. Denis Donoghue (London: Macmillan, 1972), p. 190.

14. Yeats wrote of his early days as an art student: "Our ablest student had learnt Italian to read Dante, but had never heard of Tennyson or Browning, and it was I who carried into the school some knowledge of English poetry, especially of Browning, who had begun to move me by his air of wisdom" (Au 81). In 1912 Yeats wrote to Lady Gregory about "getting up a Browning celebration" (L 565); shortly thereafter he had Ezra Pound read him *Sordello* in their Sussex cottage (Richard Ellmann, *Yeats: The Man and the Masks* [New York: Macmillan, 1948], p. 212); and in 1930 he was reading "How They Brought the Good News from Ghent to Aix" and "The Pied Piper of Hamelin" to his children (L 776).

15. *Letters to the New Island,* ed. Horace Reynolds (Cambridge: Harvard University Press, 1934), p. 98; all other quotations from this notice appear on pp. 97–99. Hereafter cited as LNI followed by page number.

16. LNI 136, 221–22; UP1 303.

17. *Browning's Essay on Shelley,* ed. Richard Garnett (London: Alexander Moring, 1903), p. 38. See UP2 131 and E&I 112 for two of Yeats's citations.

18. E&I 192. Cf. "Discoveries" (1906) in E&I 286, where Yeats still laments Browning's involvement with the world as critical rather than creative.

19. Fallis, p. 91, has a useful discussion of this passage.

20. See UP1 95, E&I 196, and L 219.

21. LNI 97, E&I 197 and 405.

22. In *Yeats* (New York: Oxford University Press, 1970), p. 486, Harold Bloom suggests that Browning was dangerous because when Yeats yielded to him he did so altogether, as in narrative poems from "How Ferencz Renyi Kept Silent" (1887) to "The Gift of Harun Al-Rashid" (1923).

23. In an influential aside from *Yeats: The Man and the Masks,* p. 172, Ellmann distinguished Browning's mask, worn toward the world but not toward the beloved, from Yeats's, worn toward both beloved and world. Bloom points out the crucial role of audience in distinguishing Browning's mask from Yeats's in his *Yeats,* pp. 331–32. See, too, Christ, pp. 37–40.

24. Predictably, Browning's rendering of the mystic alchemist Paracelsus also caught Yeats's attention. See E&I 46 and *A Vision* (New York: Macmillan, 1969), p. 9, hereafter cited as AV[B]. The remarks on Paracelsus in phase sixteen may also owe something to Browning's portrait.

25. *Explorations* (New York: Macmillan, 1962), pp. 18–19.

26. *Browning: Poetical Works 1833–1864*, ed. Ian Jack (London: Oxford University Press, 1970), p. 910, ll. 318–27.

27. Marvel Shmiefsky thinks Yeats took a more negative view of the hunter image as presenting a man "reduced to talking," in "Yeats and Browning: The Shock of Recognition," *Studies in English Literature* 10 (1970): 701–21. Shmiefsky has some interesting speculations about Yeats's response to *Paracelsus* and *Sordello,* among other works.

28. I have discussed the issues in this paragraph more fully in *Transformations of Romanticism in Yeats, Eliot, and Stevens* (Chicago: University of Chicago Press, 1976) and *The Postromantic Consciousness of Ezra Pound,* ELS Monograph Series (Victoria, B.C.: University of Victoria, 1977).

29. *Personae: Collected Shorter Poems* (London: Faber and Faber, 1952), p. 98.

CHAPTER 9

1. The manuscript is in a file marked "College" at the Pound Archive of the Collection of American Literature, the Beinecke Rare Book and Manuscript Library, Yale University. It consists of eight unpaginated sheets typed with a blue ribbon. In quotation of this and other manuscripts, I have made minor alterations of spelling and punctuation to clarify the sense.

2. *The Selected Letters of Ezra Pound,* ed. D. D. Paige (New York: New Directions, 1971), p. 218. Hereafter cited as L followed by page number.

3. Carol Christ has drawn some interesting distinctions between Pound's and Browning's use of masks, particularly the danger of self-obsession for Browning's characters versus fragmentation for Pound's. See her *Victorian and Modern Poetics* (Chicago: University of Chicago Press, 1984), pp. 41–44.

4. Not knowing which edition Pound used, I cite that published in Boston by Houghton Mifflin and Company in 1881. The remarks on "impertinent verses" and "prose-run-mad" occur on p. 329 in a discussion of Browning's poem on poetic "Popularity." I have discussed Pound's poetic use of the lines about the murex in " 'What Porridge Had John Keats?': Pound's 'L'Art' and Browning's 'Popularity,' " *Paideuma* 10 (Fall 1981): 303–6. The quotation about Tennyson, below, comes from the preface, p. x.

5. For the reader's convenience, all quotations from Browning will be from *Robert Browning: The Poems,* 2 vols., ed. John Pettigrew and Thomas J. Collins (New Haven: Yale University Press, 1981), except where there is special reason to do otherwise. Browning quoted four lines of his wife's description of Euripides as epigraph to *Balaustion's Adventure:* "Our Euripides, the human, / With his droppings of warm tears, / And his touches of things common / Till they rose to touch the spheres."

6. In the "Translations of Aeschylus" section of the essay "Translators of Greek,"

Pound states, "I have read Browning off and on for seventeen years with no small pleasure and admiration." See *Literary Essays of Ezra Pound* (New York: New Directions, 1968), p. 269; hereafter cited as LE followed by page number. Since that section of the essay was first published in *The Egoist* during 1919, 1902 seems the appropriate date for commencement of Pound's serious reading of Browning. The following quotation comes from *The Poetical Works of Robert Browning,* 2 vols. (New York: Macmillan, 1902), vol. 1, p. 661. The lines, of course, are not numbered.

7. The manuscript of "To R.B." is in the Beinecke Library as part of Pound's correspondence with Viola Baxter Jordan, where it forms one of a series of poems which he sent her from Crawfordsville, Indiana, in a letter of 24 October 1907. The following quotations in this article are taken from the manuscript, which was published without Pound's introductory note as Appendix E of Forrest Read, *'76: One World and the Cantos of Ezra Pound* (Chapel Hill: University of North Carolina Press, 1981), pp. 448–52. Because that transcript is the only published one, I note here two flaws which affect interpretation: On p. 448, the second to last line should begin "Thy lyric maid" rather than "The lyric maid" (Cowper is addressing Browning directly), and on p. 449 the seventh line should have an "of" before "Kameiros" (which denotes a place of origin). Read's commentary on pp. 65–66 taking the poem as verification of Pound's interest in the Great Seal and other arcana seems eccentric. Donald Gallup has a helpful account of the Pound-Baxter correspondence in "Ezra Pound: Letters to Viola Baxter Jordan," *Paideuma* 1 (Spring and Summer 1972): 107–11; in addition, I am grateful to him for several suggestions about pertinent manuscript materials and for help in securing copies.

8. *Personae: The Collected Shorter Poems of Ezra Pound* (New York: New Directions, 1971), p. 13. Hereafter cited as P followed by page number.

9. See Pound's essay "Chinese Poetry," *To-Day* 3 (April–May 1918): 54–57 and 93–95; the quotation is from p. 55.

10. The manuscript is in a folder marked "College: In the Water-Butt" in the Pound Archive at the Beinecke Libarary. See James Laughlin's facsimile of the story and interesting remarks on Pound's satiric streak, "Walking Around a Water-Butt," *Paris Review* No. 100 (Summer/Fall 1986): 303–18.

11. The manuscript is in a folder marked "A Lume Spento: Mesmerism" in the Pound Archive at the Beinecke Library.

12. *Collected Early Poems of Ezra Pound,* ed. Michael John King (New York: New Directions, 1976), pp. 18–19. Hereafter cited as CEP followed by page number.

13. Gallup, p. 107; the manuscript is in the Beinecke Library. In *The Spirit of Romance* (New York: New Directions, 1968), p. 16, Pound wrote, "Ovid, before Browning, raises the dead and dissects their mental processes"; hereafter cited as SR followed by page number. For a later, similar comment on the derivation of the dramatic monologue, see *ABC of Reading* (New York: New Directions, 1960), p. 78; hereafter cited as ABCR followed by page number.

14. See Chapter 3, above.

15. For a listing of the revised headings, see the Pettigrew and Collins edition, appendix 2. The best discussion is Lawrence Poston III, "Browning Rearranges Browning," *Studies in Browning and His Circle* 2 (1974): 39–54.

16. Pound particularly stressed Browning's Italian exile during his own domicile in

Rapallo. Two examples occur in ABCR 132–33 and "The Jefferson-Adams Letters," reprinted in *Selected Prose, 1909–1965,* ed. William Cookson (New York: New Directions, 1973), p. 158.

17. *Gaudier-Brzeska: A Memoir* (New York: New Directions, 1970), p. 85; hereafter cited as GB followed by page number.

18. "Chinese Poetry," p. 94.

19. I have discussed these views of Pound's masks during this period in *The Postromantic Consciousness of Ezra Pound,* ELS Monograph Series (Victoria, B.C.: University of Victoria, 1977).

20. Among discussions of the relation of Pound's dramatic monologues to Browning's, the three most helpful are N. Christoph de Nagy, *The Poetry of Ezra Pound: The Pre-Imagist Stage,* rev. ed. (Bern: Francke Verlag, 1968), ch. 5, reprinted in shortened form as "Pound and Browning" in *New Approaches to Ezra Pound,* ed. Eva Hesse (Berkeley: University of California Press, 1969); Hugh Witemeyer, *The Poetry of Ezra Pound: Forms and Renewal, 1908–1920* (Berkeley: University of California Press, 1969), pp. 60–86; and Carol Christ (see above, n. 3).

21. The manuscript of this unpublished letter is in the Pound Archive of the Beinecke Library. It has been quoted from by Myles Slatin both in "A History of Pound's Cantos I–XVI, 1915–1925," *American Literature* 35 (1963–64): 183–95, and in his fine, unpublished dissertation " 'Mesmerism': A Study of Ezra Pound's Use of the Poetry of Robert Browning" (Yale, 1957), and by Ronald Bush in the helpful third chapter of *The Genesis of Ezra Pound's Cantos* (Princeton: Princeton University Press, 1976); I am indebted to all three works.

22. *Poetry: A Magazine of Verse* 10 (1917): 113–21, 180–88, and 248–54. Further quotations from *Three Cantos* will be identified by their page number in *Poetry* enclosed in parentheses within the text. The manuscript drafts of *Three Cantos* cited in this essay are in the Pound Archive at the Beinecke Library.

23. Pettigrew and Collins, vol. 1, p. 152.

24. The best discussion of these three points is in Bush, *Genesis,* ch. 3.

25. "Pound and the *Cantos:* 'Ply over Ply,' " *Paideuma* 8 (Fall 1979): 229–35.

26. See Michael F. Harper, "Truth and Calliope: Ezra Pound's Malatesta," *PMLA* 96 (1981): 86–103, and Peter D'Epiro, *A Touch of Rhetoric: Ezra Pound's Malatesta Cantos* (Ann Arbor: UMI Research Press, 1983). Jonathan Ward's "Pound's Browning and the Issue of 'Historical Sense,' " *Browning Society Notes* 15 (1985): 10–28, was published at the same time as the original version of the present essay and contains an interesting discussion of Browning and Pound against the context of nineteenth-century historiography.

27. L 257, 308, 313, 8; for the letter to Viola Baxter, see above, note 7.

28. Here I am thinking of the work of Harold Bloom and his followers from *The Anxiety of Influence* (New York: Oxford University Press, 1973) onwards, as well as some of my own suggestions in *Transformations of Romanticism in Yeats, Eliot, and Stevens* (Chicago: University of Chicago Press, 1976). Not surprisingly, Bloom has little use for Pound.

29. "Ezra Pound," in *Poetry: A Magazine of Verse* 68 (1946): 337–38.

Index

Abd-El-Kadr, 27

Abercrombie, Lascelles, 125

Abrams, M. H., 19, 39, 54

Adams, Henry, *The Education of Henry Adams,* 48

Aeschylus, 81, 140

Agricola, Johannes, 26

Andrewes, Lancelot, *Nativity Sermon,* 48

Aristophanes, 130, 138

Arnold, Matthew, 39, 48–49; mentioned, 3, 40, 46–47, 50, 118; "Dover Beach," 39, 43; "Introduction" to *The Study of Celtic Literature,* 112; "The Scholar-Gypsy," 24, 39, 43–45

Balzac, Honoré de, 91

Barry, Iris, 140

Bartolommeo, Fra, 30

Baxter, Viola, 133, 140, 157 n. 7

Beardsley, Aubrey, 79

Beaumont, Sir George, 20

Benson, A. C., *Edward FitzGerald,* 48

Berkeley, George (Bishop), 118

Binyon, Laurence, 140

Blake, William, 73–76, 78–81; mentioned, 7–8, 55, 57, 69, 96, 97, 101–2, 107, 112, 114; *Book of*

Urizen, 65, 92; *Milton,* 66; *Songs of Innocence and of Experience,* 9

Bloom, Harold, 64, 155 n. 22

Book of Matthew, 34

Bright, Michael H., 147 nn. 1, 5

Browning, Elizabeth Barrett, 133; *Wine of Cyprus,* 127

Browning, Robert, 3–6, 9–11, 15–29 passim, 30–37 passim, 106–22 passim, 123–41 passim; mentioned, 40, 48, 50, 77; "Abt Vogler," 37, 38–39, 45–46; "Andrea del Sarto," 30, 126; *Aristophanes' Apology,* 124, 127, 129–30, 138; "Artemis Prologuizes," 16–17, 22–23, 26; *Balaustion's Adventure,* 124, 127–31, 134, 138; "Boot and Saddle" (formerly "My Wife Gertrude"), 16, 18–19; "Camp and Cloister," 16–17, 21–22; "Cavalier Tunes," 16–19, 23, 27, 29; "Cleon," 133–34; "Count Gismond" (formerly "France"), 16–17, 19–22, 25–26; "Cristina," 16, 24–25; "A Death in the Desert," 133; *Dramatic Lyrics* (1842), 10, 15–29, 134; *Dramatic Romances and Lyrics* (1845), 15; *Dramatic Romances and Lyrics* (1849), 25; *Dramatis Personae,* 15; "The Englishman in Italy," 47; "Essay on

DATE DUE